Critical Views on Selman-Troytt

"If God had not meant us to keep concealed our nether regions, then he would not have given us clothes. I call upon God to strike this sinner dead . . ." *Sunderland Temperance Chronicle*, 1897

"I feel I shall never again soil myself without believing that I should be recording the matter for posterity . . . Jeremy has managed to turn a commonplace event into a *cause celèbre*." OSCAR WILDE, 1892

"It can be nothing less than a blasphemy before God when any man deliberately flings the contents of his trousers in the public's face . . ." *The Glasgow Herald*, 1892

"It would be fair to say that before Selman-Troytt people had little or no knowledge of their own bodies. It took Selman-Troytt to make people aware of their sexuality, just as it had taken Shakespeare to make them aware of their humanity three hundred years earlier."
PROFESSOR SERGEI MINSKOV, Minskov Institute of Stimulus, Kursk, 2007

"Mr. Selman-Troytt's account of his first nocturnal emission made me weep." JETHRO TULL III, *The Evesham Seed Drill Advertiser*, 1898

"Mr. Selman-Troytt appears to believe that I can have an interest in the interior of his undergarments. Allow me to disabuse him of such a notion immediately. I have no interest even in my own; nor should any man, even in the cause of scientific investigation, inquire too closely into that which should pass before Our Lord alone." *The Spectator*, 1892

"All men may soil themselves but only a very select few will have the grace and wit to express their experience with the breath-taking charm of Mr. Selman-Troytt." *The Times*, 1892

"Whilst I concur heartily with the philosophy which is expressed so eruditely by Mr. Selman-Troytt, and although I sympathise with his very necessary examination of the subject matter, nevertheless I feel I must criticise him upon one point of style: to wit his tendency, or penchant, for prolixity, and his occasional divergence, even meandering, into pleonasm." JOHN RUSKIN, 1894

"Selman-Troytt's prose is like a softened petal dropped into a gentle, fragrant stream and then left to meander its natural course through the verdant topography of our senses. It finds its way without strain or difficulty, bringing to bear upon our faculties only the gentle erosion required to implant itself within our memories like a softly-cut valley. Whenever I read him I feel dangerously spiritual, as though my soul were in danger of imminent salvation. Invariably, I am driven to smoke a cigarette immediately afterwards, to transport me away from the divine and back into decadence." OSCAR WILDE, 1894

"Mr. Selman-Troytt is a papist heretic with no right to life. Our readers cry: 'Burn this spawn of Beelzebub!'" *The Belfast Echo*, 1899

"Mr. Selman-Troytt is a cheap sensationalist! A publicity hound of the first water! Why, I've soiled my trousers a score of times and never thought to commit it to paper! I've also ejaculated both prematurely and nocturnally. In short, much that has happened to this man has happened to me, yet did I decide to set it down on paper and generate from it a significant income and a legion of sycophantic acolytes in a cheap and vulgar display of publicity-seeking fervour redolent of the most meretricious harlot? No! I commend you: **Do not buy any of this man's books.**" *The Weekly Literary Periodical*, 1909

The Selman-Troytt Papers

BEING THE SELECTED LETTERS, JOURNALS AND PUBLISHED WORKS OF JEREMY SELMAN-TROYTT (1868–1916), THE RENOWNED VICTORIAN PIONEER OF SEXUAL HEALTH AND HYGIENE, AND INVENTOR OF NUMEROUS CONTRAPTIONS BEAUTIFUL IN CONCEPTION IF NOT ALWAYS EFFICACIOUS...

Edited by

P. J. Barrington B.A. (Mull)

First published in 2007 by
Old Street Publishing Ltd, 28–32 Bowling Green Lane,
London EC1R 0BJ, UK

www.oldstreetpublishing.co.uk

ISBN-13: 978-1-905847-20-4

1 3 5 7 9 10 8 6 4 2

A CIP catalogue record for this book is available
from the British Library.

Designed and typeset by Patty Rennie

Printed and bound by J. H. Haynes & Co. Ltd., Sparkford

Dedication

In memory of Major-General Gavin Mitchell, KCB DSO, a pioneering Scot reputed to have made many of the first solo ascents in Glencoe between 1880 and 1896. He was an individualist, often climbing without equipment if he considered the climb to be 'Naught but a wee tweeds-and-brogues ramble' - a description he applied to most Scottish ascents. He refused to record his own climbing feats, opining that 'only a pompous sodomite would ever dream of doing so', and for this reason had many violent debates with Sir Hugh Thomas Munro, the first person to compile a list all Scottish mountains above 3000 feet. Mitchell described this work as 'an excellent substitute for lavatory paper on a long climb'.

Lancrannoch from Lochnagar by Hugh Munro, showing his favourite bothy (at left)
Courtesy of the Rannoch Mountaineering Club collection

Munro was a founder member of the Scottish Mountaineering Club (1889), but Mitchell had nothing but scorn for the club and could often be found outside the premises, screaming abuse at those within. The relationship between the two men was strange, in that Munro clearly had a grudging respect for Mitchell, while Mitchell had none at all for Munro and abused him openly whenever they met. Munro never retaliated publicly, but on the occasions when Mitchell was a guest at Munro's Lindertis Estate, Munro would never allow him to take fruit into his room.

Mitchell's unassailable optimism lingers on in the Scottish psyche. In the misted valleys of Glencoe his thundering cry of 'Go Rannoch!' still echoes in the frosty air.

Contents

Ante-Matter

PART ONE - The Soiling Years

PART TWO - THE ROMANTIC YEARS

PART THREE - The Sexual Years

Appendectomies

Introduction

by

Professor Reginald L'Ampere

I was both honoured and delighted to be asked to select extracts from the works of Jeremy Selman-Troytt. However, I must confess that whilst I was excited by the opportunity to re-read his wonderful manuscripts, I was simultaneously daunted by the task of having to edit and reject so much marvellous material. This is a problem with which all students of Selman-Troytt will be familiar, for his output was, quite literally, astonishing. A single volume of his would fill this book several times over, and it should be borne in mind that he numbered 89 volumes among the one hundred and fifty thousand or so pages that he published between 1886 and his tragic death in 1916.

For this anthology I have chosen excerpts from his full-length case-studies, from his varied monographs, from his private journals and from his personal correspondence in the hope that, in concert, they may produce a more detailed portrait of the genius behind such a prodigious talent.

Jeremy Selman-Troytt was born in 1868, seventeenth child of an extremely wealthy London family whose fortune had been made in the manufacture of glazier's putty following the Great Fire of London in 1666. His father, Josiah, and grand-father, Joshua, both hailed from Market Harborough, where their commercial and manufacturing reputation was such that a bargain struck in the market-place was often described as being '*as hard as Troytt putty*'.

Josiah, a headstrong and vigorous man, moved the company headquarters to London in the spring of 1846. With characteristic single-mindedness, he then, within twenty-seven days, courted and married the glazing heiress Lady Bethany Twirler, capturing both her attention and her heart by sending her a gigantic facsimile of her favourite pet spaniel, hand-fashioned from cast iron and flame-hardened putty by workers at the Selman-Troytt Manufactory. At over eighteen feet (c. 6 metres) in height and weighing over nine tonnes, it was indeed a princely tribute and caused Lady Bethany to quip: '*I will not know which is the real one until one of them licks my hand. I shall then know that the other is the model. Also, one is bigger than the other and that will help me discriminate. Failing those two tests I shall call out and the one that heeds my summons will be alive. My final resort will be to strike them both upon the snout. The one that does not reverberate will be the real dog.*'

Their union represented not only a sound business merger but the coupling of two hearts, and she bore him children continuously for twenty-five years, undergoing an astounding thirty-two confinements.

Their oldest surviving son, Jonah, with the assistance of his brothers John and Jonas, took on the responsibilities of the family firm early in 1870 in order to allow his parents the freedom to pursue their hobbies in a carefree retirement. Jonah (who from a very early age had asked the question: '*How hard can making putty be?!*') was a fantastic success. Between 1871 and 1887 he was responsible for a quadrupling of Britain's putty production in real terms, producing thereby a surplus which could be exported to all parts of the Empire. In the meantime, his father produced a constant stream of miniature cigar boxes inlaid with exquisite marquetry, while his mother embroidered over two thousand samplers bearing the Selman-Troytt motto: *Per Vitrum Ad Fortunam**.

With such commercially enterprising forebears already *in situ*, and with academic honours for the family already being pursued by various of the middle children such as Joseph (Eton), Jasper (Oxon.), and Jonty (Cantab.), Jeremy was not expected to function at any level of proficiency – whether physical or intellectual – beyond that expected of a gentleman of leisure. Accordingly, he was never sent to school, and received no formal education whatsoever beyond a three month spell with a private tutor at the age of twelve. Sadly, Jeremy's talent did not distinguish itself by its precocity and even these lessons were

* Scholars are generally in agreement that the finest translation of the Selman-Troytt motto is that of Prof. Ivan Cutlass of Marlborough College: "Prosperity Through Glass".

abandoned when his father discovered during an impromptu oral examination over dinner that his son had neither Latin nor Greek, and indeed was so weak at mathematics that an angry Selman-Troytt *père* was moved to exclaim: '*T'lad couldn't even combine two bags of putty in a bath!*'

But Jeremy took a different view of this failed attempt to lift him onto the first rung of literacy, and was so inspired by the final words of his departing tutor – '*Believe no man who calls you a fool – even if he knows you as well as I do*' – that he underwent a period of intensive self-education which began with reading skills acquired from surreptitious glances into old copies of *The Lancet*, made when his father's back was turned. This choice of reading matter – although totally inadvertent – was to engender two significant changes within the developing child: it was to foster a fascination with science and investigation which continued unabated until his untimely death at the age of only forty-eight; furthermore, it provided a depth of specialisation which meant that he could, from the age of seventeen onwards and in theory at least, perform amputations and other major surgery.

As a Victorian, Selman-Troytt saw that the purpose of education was moral improvement, but he was also heavily influenced by the pioneering spirit of technological and scientific progress that gripped the age. Both factors are very evident in his work. His writings display a fascination (one might even say a *passion*) with all topics from the monumental to the trivial, in particular those which involve a direct connection with himself. In a period that inspired many auto-observers, Selman-Troytt was pre-eminent. During that golden age of discovery and 'wonderment', when the dedicated 'amateur' could still discourse on level terms with the learned professional, what distinguishes Selman-Troytt from his peers is not only his unflagging enthusiasm but also his diligent application even in the face of personal hardship. No change within his body escaped his scrutiny, no event was deemed too insignificant to record, and no detail was considered inconsequential if it might instruct others.

Selman-Troytt was crushed by falling masonry in 1916.

Professor Reginald L'Ampere
Emeritus Professor of English, University of Helsingborg

A Selman-Troytt Timeline

Date	Jeremy Selman-Troytt's Life
1865	
1868	Jeremy Selman-Troytt is born to the brutal glazing magnate, Josiah Selman-Troytt (see p.11). From the age of 4 Jeremy shows an aversion to glass which infuriates his father.
1876	
1878	Bored with sitting at home doing nothing, JS-T slowly begins to direct his own education. Tentatively, but then with increasing confidence, he begins a correspondence with the leading thinkers, scientists and political figures of the day (see e.g. pp. 5,41,78,97).
1878	Selman-Troytt Glazing, already one of the biggest companies in England, begins a push towards creating a monopoly in the United Kingdom. The immense wealth produced by the company will subsidise JS-T's lifestyle and fund much of his later research.
1882	After experimenting on the household staff JS-T determines upon a life of scientific research. He starts his own journal (p.7) which he maintains ceaselessly until his death. It is the start of an intense study of himself which will absorb him for the rest of his life. His father becomes more brutal.
1886	JS-T performs his first (unlicensed) haemorrhoidectomy.
1887	JS-T publishes first monograph: *Methodology of Acute Auto-Observation*

Scientific Context	Historical Events
Abraham Lincoln (American) assassinated. Failed attempts to clean the blood from his clothes prompt new research into stain removal agents.	
Alfred Nobel (Swedish) invents dynamite, losing both hands in the process.	
	Battle of the Little Big Horn
Pierre Rochemel (French) designs and builds the world's first mechanical prepuce retractor. A floor-standing model, it is an instant success. He is feted all over Europe.	First riveted jeans sold to miners by Levi Strauss
Alexander Graham Bell (Scottish) invents the telephone and uses it to call Rochemel and order a prepuce retractor.	
Thomas Edison (American) invents the record player just months after it has been invented by someone else. The first record in history is scratched by his assistant.	Phoenix Park Murders take place in Dublin
Thomas Edison (American) invents the light bulb only a year after it has been patented in England by Joseph Swan.	

Date	Jeremy Selman-Troytt's Life
1887	JS-T becomes increasingly fascinated by ailments, particularly those of the wealthy. His first social relationships are with sick and enfeebled people who seek his opinions (see e.g. pp.92-96).
1892	JS-T achieves considerable notoriety with his sixth publication: *The First Time I Soiled My Trousers* (see pp.21,35). Many more of the ailing and confused begin to seek his advice, even though he is without formal qualifications.
1893	Father now very brutal indeed.
1895	JS-T begins experiments with prosthetics by carving replacement limbs from ivory (see e.g. p.92).
1896	JS-T proposes a cure for spatulitis, the uncontrolled widening of the distal phalanges of the hands suffered by typists. His cure involves the use of thin prosthetic finger extensions made from ivory.

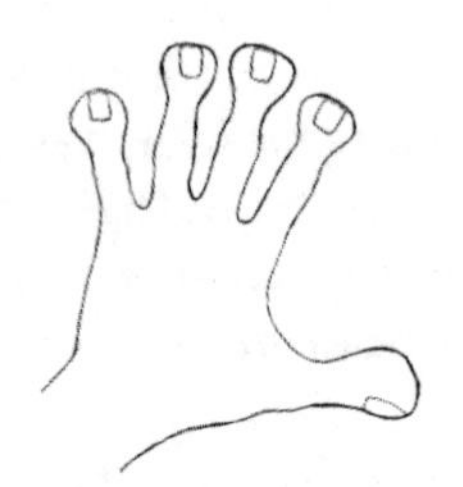

Date	Jeremy Selman-Troytt's Life
1898	JS-T experiences his first nocturnal emission and publishes an account of it (see p.69). It is an instant bestseller and his consulting practice enlarges. Encouraged, he embarks on a search for a wife and begins a series of high-profile liaisons. He is increasingly the recipient of death threats by political and religious extremists.
1899	Winston Churchill consults JS-T over persistent balanitis following his escape from a Boer prison camp and subsequent visit to a brothel in Laurenço Marques
1905	JS-T becomes very excited by George Oenslager's acceleration of the rubber vulcanisation process. He produces a pair of vulcanised rubber trousers but they are too stiff for practical use.

Thomas Edison (American) invents the contact lens only one year after Swiss ophthalmologist, Dr Frick.

Thomas Hardy (English) publishes *Jude the Obscure* but readers are scandalised by Hardy's fictional accounts of Jude's trouser soiling. They consider him to be treating the subject with levity. Hardy removes the offending passages but the damage is already done. Critics label the book 'Jude the Obscene' and sales plummet. Hardy is mortified and never writes another novel.

Oscar Wilde (Irish) convicted of sodomy. Lumière Bros. (French) try to buy the film rights to the trial from Wilde's wife.

Roentgen (German) discovers x-rays. He gives enthusiastic demonstrations all over Europe, amazing and exciting audiences with 'live' pictures of his internal organs. He becomes the first person to die from radiation poisoning.

Koenig Vaysoff (American) invents the 'hotdog', a combination of wurst and bread. Millions are eaten. He becomes wealthy.

Surgoaad and Tostov (Swedish) try to prove that impotence is a state of mind. Under hypnosis, Surgoaad remains erect for 9 days 14 hrs 37 mins. When he is finally 'awakened' by Tostov, he passes out.

Boer Wars begin. Pierre Rochemel dies quietly in Paris, his floor-standing prepuce retractor all but forgotten.

Date	Jeremy Selman-Troytt's Life
1907	JS-T experiences his first involuntary ejaculation and publishes account to critical acclaim (see p.117). His consulting practice enlarges and diverges.
1908	JS-T offers first consultation on erectile dysfunction (see e.g. pp.158-165).
1909	A life-long frustration with the restrictive nature of normal joint-articulations culminates in his first abstract thesis *Speculations Upon Improbable Joint Articulations* (see p.147).
1909	W. G. Grace consults Jeremy over his persistent failure to bring his wife (Agnes née Day) to orgasm. Jeremy suggests a new method of labial stimulation and publishes the case as a monograph. Grace is subsequently barred from membership of the M.C.C.
1912	Intense research pays dividends when JS-T discovers that lanolin can soften seed pods.
1914	
1915	JS-T opens his personal collection of dermal flakes to the public for a two-week exhibition.
1916	JS-T publishes *Social and Sexual Etiquette* (see p.187) in an effort to help readers reduce the shame and humiliation of physical congress.
1916	On 5th November 1916 Jeremy Selman-Troytt dies under falling masonry (see p.208). The birth control campaigner Mary Stopes delivers the eulogy at his funeral, declaring in public that she would have consented to congress with Selman-Troytt had he offered to wear a sheath.
1917	

Chuck Lydon (American) invents the 'Power Lunch', a meal that does not need to be chewed. Americans can now eat in their cars during the journey to the end of their driveways to collect their morning paper. It is a huge seller and he becomes wealthy.

Proust (French) begins writing *À la recherche du temps perdu*. It is almost finished in 1922, when he suddenly loses interest.

C. Herbert de Melville III (American) designs a big sandwich which he calls 'Big Sandwich'. It sells well and his wealth increases.

Thomas Edison (American) discovers the proton only three months after Ernest Rutherford (English).

The US. Surgeon General reports that obesity among U.S. citizens now affects 68% of the population.

Great War starts

Hoping to increase his fortune, Thomas Edison (American) begins work on 'inventing' a prepuce retractor for obese people who have lost sight of their genitals.

Einstein (Swiss) publishes *General Theory of Relativity.*

War Office equips British front line troops with JS-T's vulcanised trousers to protect them on their walk across *no man's land*. Slowed by the trousers, many are shot in the upper torso.

America enters the Great War, prolonging it by a year.

PART ONE

The Soiling Years

1868–1896

Jeremy Selman-Troytt 1868–1916

At the age of three years (left) riding a tricycle that was always described as a present from 'Grandada Joshua', even though Joshua Selman-Troytt* had been deceased for twenty-two years by the time Jeremy was born.

By a remarkable and unpleasant twist of fate, Jeremy was riding the very same tricycle on the day of his death forty-five years later. Subsequently the tricycle was rejected by the Selman-Troytt family, none of whom would chance to ride it. Eventually it was given to some poor people.

Jeremy at the age of twenty-one (right), shortly after performing a haemorrhoidectomy at the request of his cousin Jeffrey**, who was willing to trust the young Jeremy when all others scoffed at him openly. Although the operation was not a success, and his cousin was never able to sit again, Jeremy was always grateful for the boost it gave to his confidence and later wrote that it had provided the impetus for further research and practice.

---

* See p.10. Further information on the entire Selman-Troytt family can be obtained from the Introduction on p.xvii and the Selman-Troytt Timeline on p.xx.

** See p.56 for a short biography of Jeffrey Selman-Troytt.

THOMAS APPLEBY B.A. (OXON.)
TUTOR IN THE HUMANITIES,
27 EVESHAM PLACE, PUTNEY, W.

Josiah Selman-Troytt,
14 Berkeley Square,
London, W.

20 February, 1880

Dear Mr. Selman-Troytt,

I have this day the greatest of pleasures in expressing my intense gratitude that you have decided to entrust your son's tutelage to my care.

Although the appointment has come as a surprise considering the accusations you made about me during my interview, I am pleased to have the opportunity to prove you wrong about those aspects of my character. I pray that I shall, and that you will have no cause to regret your decision to place Jeremy's intellectual welfare in my hands. I find myself excited at the prospect of guiding him through his letters, and beyond them into an exploration of the classics.

The boy has impressed me much, if not in present academic wealth then at least in enthusiasm. At his meeting with me his eyes darted wildly, abstractedly and excitedly when he began to consider the prospect of acquiring an education. Although he is but twelve years of age he showed me a huge bundle of letters which he described as 'the start of a lifetime's correspondence with the world's greatest thinkers'. I regard this as a very encouraging sign, even though at present his correspondents are patently imaginary and the pages were simply covered in patterns of irregular loops.* Whilst the boy has a poor writing hand now, I feel confident that I can guarantee to you that within a month of my arrival he will be ready to write to a real person.

* See Appendix II on p.241 for a facsimile showing Selman-Troytt's early writing style.

Again, Sir, I proffer my thanks for your confidence in my abilities and your stated assurances that you believe I will not interfere with your son physically. You are correct; I will not.

Ever your most humble and obedient servant,
Thos. Appleby B.A. (Oxon.)

THOMAS APPLEBY B.A. (OXON.)
TUTOR IN THE HUMANITIES,
14 BERKELEY SQUARE, LONDON, W.

Josiah Selman-Troytt,
14 Berkeley Square,
London, W.

20 May, 1880

Sir!

I tender my resignation forthwith. I shall depart your house today and not return. My luggage and effects should be forwarded in care of Mrs Appleby, 11 Brighton Terrace, Putney.

I hope I never see you again, and I express my sympathy and my horror that your son should have to continue residing under the same roof as you. That you should have fathered sixteen other children beggars belief. My concerns rest heartily with your wife.

Were it not for the unshakable conviction that you would treat my request with scorn and derision, I would ask that you care well for the boy Jeremy, for he is a well-intentioned child and could achieve some little measure of academic progress beyond the start I have given him, his physical appearance, intelligence and emotional disposition notwithstanding.

But what point is there in communicating this to such as you, who would as readily crush a nightingale to determine its resistance to impact as harken to the beauty of its song? I would be employed more gainfully in attempting to teach a pig to shave without a looking-glass. You are a knave! And what is worse is that I think you to be unaware of the fact, since you consider your behaviour to be acceptable even when it resides beyond the bounds of Christian decency!

I have not yet determined whether to visit my local constabulary. If my luggage does not follow me immediately, or is found to have been tampered with, then I certainly shall.

You are no Christian!
Thos. Appleby B.A. (Oxon.)

J. SELMAN-TROYTT, ESQ.,
14 BERKELEY SQUARE, LONDON, W.

Rt. Hon. B. Disraeli,
Hughenden Manor,
High Wycombe,
Buckinghamshire

27 March, 1881

Dear Mr. Disraeli,*

I hope you are well. I am well.

Thank you for answering my questions. Father said you would.

I enjoyed your letter very much, but please let me make a small correction without making you angry. I hope! You write on page 2: '. . .and this will have been done, undoubtedly, at the moment of your

* This is the first extant example of Selman-Troytt's correspondence with a real person, composed using legible letters and words.

circumcision . . .', whilst on page 7 you write: 'it is possible that your mother will have crocheted a yarmulke for you'. From both of the above I think that you think I am Jewish. I am not. I am a Christian. Cook says that being a Christian will test the faith of all intelligent men now that Mr. Darwin has told everyone that some of us are descended from an ape. Anyway, what I want to tell you is that my foreskin is intact . . . which means, I am afraid, that the advice you give on page 4 would not apply to me. I apologise for carrying this bad news to you and hope that you will not become angry with me.

Also, it means that I cannot provide the information you request in the passage that ends: '. . . so George and I have never encountered an infected glans among those who have undergone circumcision. Does the condition of your own glans bear this out?' I am sorry about this and hope you will not be angry with me.

It was very kind of you to send me a collection of your novels, but I have decided to return them to you as I am very unlikely to read them. Although I read a lot now I never read works of fiction because I have very little time and prefer to use it for something interesting. Therefore I should never read your books, even though you say that they are 'the best novels in Christendom'. I apologise. However, I have heard that they are not good to read, so I feel comforted that my loss is not significant. Being Jewish, you will understand my need to prioritise ruthlessly.

Your most obedient servant,
Jeremy Selman-Troytt

Post Script: Sorry, I forgot some. Yes, I do like cats very much. They are nice to stroke. We had a cat but Father had it killed, as you know, because you were there.

JOURNAL NOTES FOR FEBRUARY 17TH, 1884

I have decided to start a journal so that in this, my sixteenth year, I can begin to record the miscellany of ideas and questions that course through my brain in a single day. Always so many questions. Cook says I ask too many questions, but I am not sure. I asked Father about this but he treated me to one of his prolonged silences and then struck me a blow to the chin with a muttered oath.

I am determined to begin my explorations as soon as I have research materials at my disposal. In the meantime I shall take note of the first subjects that will occupy my study:

— Why do knees bend only in one direction? Surely they would be of greater value if they articulated in all directions?*

— Why does pain hurt? When I am punched how comes the pain to be there? Is it a gathering of some black humour at the site of the contusion that causes the bruise?

— Is Father correct in his assertion that wearing a pair of canvas gaiters will prevent varicose veins?

JOURNAL NOTES FOR FEBRUARY 18TH, 1884

The second day of my journal. Father had a meeting in the house last night. A lot of important people came. Many had thin legs and bulbous noses. I asked one man why his nose was bulbous and Father struck me. Another man with a bulbous nose interfered and Father struck him. Mother tried to calm him by humming.

* See p.147 for Selman-Troytt's mature attempt to redesign the knee.

Hennessy called today and asked me what I knew about ectoplasm.

I have thought again about knees but cannot guess the answer. I will continue with this.

I was thinking this afternoon about washing. Are there people who wash themselves? Fairbanks always washes me but who washes Fairbanks? And who washes the person who washes Fairbanks? And who washes the person who washes the person who washes Fairbanks? &c. &c. I thought about this but it very quickly grew into a big tangle whose ends I could not keep in my head and I had to let it escape before it overwhelmed me. I became a little frightened. I distracted myself by visiting the kitchen and feeding a few scraps of uncooked pastry to the boot boy to see if it would make him ill. It did, which is very interesting. I think I shall begin recording such things to see if such study can lead to conclusions.

I should one day like to be regarded as a great man of science. Science intrigues me and excites me like no other subject. My brain is awash with thousands of questions.

Journal Notes for August 17th, 1885

I have today read the most marvellous account* of an extraordinary engine which has quite determined me upon a study of the genitals. I am intrigued to learn the correlation of the principal physical parts and should be fascinated to attempt a device of my own.

---

* Almost certainly this refers to a description of Rochemel's work on a floor-standing prepuce retractor. See Appendix III(a) on p.242.

Perhaps I can prevail upon Father for funding? I am convinced that I should be able to reduce the weight considerably, perhaps to as little as 50 lbs (22.7kg), so that the entire contrivance should become portable. Perhaps it could be housed inside a suitcase for convenience. In that way a gentleman could carry it about his person at all times so as to have it available when required. I am so excited by this that I can barely sleep! I shall begin some preliminary designs tomorrow. In the meantime I shall inform Fairbanks that I require his genitals for study and experimentation.

Journal Notes for August 18th, 1885

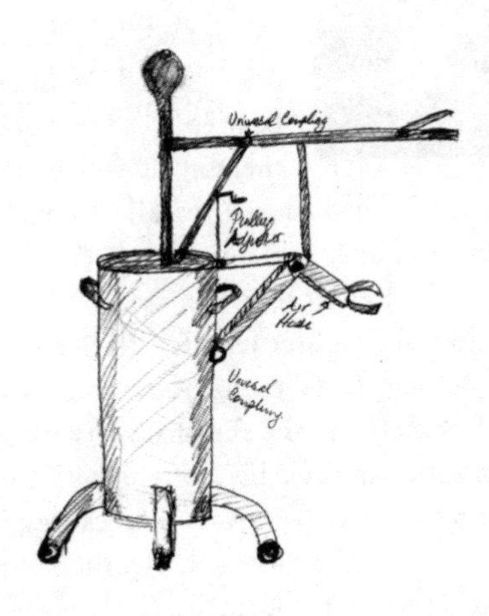

I have tried to reconstruct an image of the original retractor from Terchad's description but it is *very* difficult. The technical details are scant and it is difficult to construct them into a cohesive mental image. I find it is easier to see things when they are before my eyes, rather than behind them. I believe it may look like the above, but I cannot be sure, which makes me feel uncertain.

Family

Joshua Selman-Troytt 1790–1846

A unique nitrogen-stabilised daguerreotype of Jeremy's paternal grandfather, taken by George Beard – holder of the British patent for the daguerreotype process – only seconds before the kiln explosion in which Joshua was killed. Beard himself was slightly injured in the blast, and subsequently charged double for developing the plate.

Joshua's four children, conceived in a brief period of intense sexual activity between 1819 and 1821, blamed themselves for his death – particularly Josiah, the oldest, who had caused the kiln to explode. However, the relationship between father and only son had not been a close one – they communicated rarely, other than via notes on small scraps of paper. In his hysterical daughter Jennifer, Joshua's sudden death caused stress-induced dermatitis (the first case officially recorded at St Bartholomew's hospital) and she shedded regularly thereafter.

The fatal explosion saturated his clothing with flammable linseed oil, causing him to smoulder on for nearly a week despite being left in the open and regularly doused with water. His funeral date was finally set only after an inspection by the local fire brigade.

Joshua's unexpected death paved the way for Josiah, considerably more ruthless and ambitious than his father, to begin expanding the family firm in ways his father had never even considered.*

---

* An analysis of the Selman-Troytt family's monopolisation of the British glazing industry, their manipulation of the financial markets, and their attempts to dominate glazing worldwide, are contained in the well-known essay *The 'Glazing Wars' – Economic Causes & Geo-Political Effects* by Finlay Finlayson. A small part of this work appears in Appendix VI on p.269.

Family

Josiah Selman-Troytt 1820–1918

This is one of only four extant photographs of Jeremy's father, Josiah, who refused steadfastly to be '*photo-ed*' until he was well into his sixties because of a fixed belief that it would steal away his soul.

Josiah suffered under lifelong anti-Semitic prejudice, even though he was not Jewish. However his protestations as to his Anglo-Saxon ancestry fell upon deaf ears among those convinced by such an apparently Jewish surname. In reality his mediaeval forebears had been Christian fishmongers whose frequent market cries of "salmon and trout" were adopted as a patronymic epithet by their contemporaries. Thus, the Domesday Book contains the entry: '*Jenwald Salemane-Troutte holds land from Geoffroi de Caen* . . .'. Josiah had these details printed in a pamphlet which he handed to new acquaintances along with a cigar and a putty catalogue, but still he could not gain admittance to White's Club*. Those inside raised their glasses in jeering toasts of derision, hurled ribald remarks through the windows and told him to seek the company of his '*sheeny friends like Disraeli*', while Josiah was left to fume and expectorate on the pavement.

Increasingly embittered and vicious, he sought refuge in the

* The famous Gentleman's Club in St James's, London.

manufacture of miniature cigar boxes, none of which was over an inch in length. To this pursuit he devoted almost eighteen hours a day for over thirty years. Eventually he died.

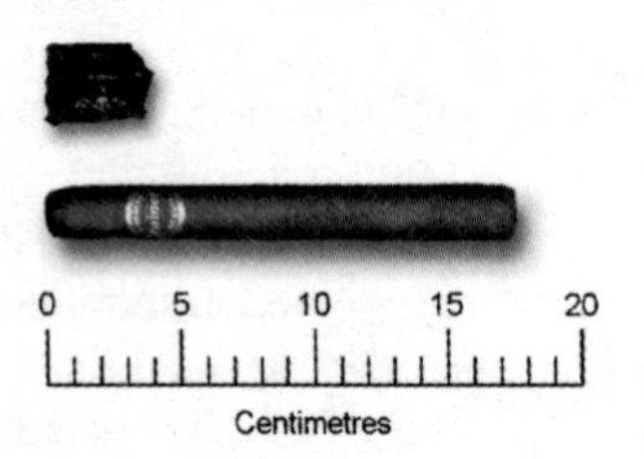

An entry (left) from a 1936 copy of Jellicoe's auction catalogue showing the exquisite marquetry that Josiah employed in the manufacture of his miniature cigar boxes. This example sold for just over £11,000 to a wealthy Argentinean smoker who bought the box as an anniversary present for his Patagonian wife, also a heavy smoker. As a romantic conceit he had it filled with miniature cigars, custom-made in Havana.

Family

Lady Bethany Twirler 1826–1927

Lady Bethany was a justifiably renowned beauty when Josiah surprised London society by winning her heart. To their union she brought an impressive dowry of 25,000 panes of glass – variously sized – and 4 cwt.* of sprigs.**

In the following years she devoted herself exclusively to childbirth, sampler embroidery and lace-making – often combining all three activities.

She is pictured (right) in 1874, with her eldest son Jonah† and grandson James‡. Lady Bethany made not only the child's smock but also the tassels on the arms of the chair. Poignantly, her diary entry for that day records: '*Made eighty-seven tassels . . . four more than yesterday.*'

---

* Four hundredweight is equal to 203.2kg.

** Glazing nails

† See p. 84.

‡ See p. 84 again.

Journal Notes for June 3rd, 1886

Letter from Joseph*. It is an inconvenience to be interrupted in the midst of my research but I felt compelled to read it in case someone had died. However, it was the opposite type of news. Mary is with child, and Joseph believes it will be a baby boy. Mary wants to christen it Judas but Father has refused permission and threatened to cut Joseph off or even to strike the child when it is born if she perseveres in this course. Father's suggestion is Japheth, which means apparently 'May he expand' or 'Engorgement' but Joseph is worried about how Mary will pronounce it with her lisp. Joseph's wish is to call the boy Jesus. He plans to register the child for Eton by telegram as soon as the umbilicus is cut.

Journal Notes for February 11th, 1887

I decided to walk to the tobacconist's in Piccadilly for some Turkish cigarettes. Thighs and knees chafed. I shall not venture out again unless absolutely necessary.

Journal Notes for May 23rd, 1887

The physical effects of the belladonna extract are quite shocking. Mouth drier. My septum seems to be expanding widthways and my nostrils are almost closed. Breathing laboured and difficult, but senses seem more acute. I am much more aware of dust on ledges and other horizontal surfaces, and smells have changed identity.

---

* One of Jeremy's older brothers. See p.55.

J. SELMAN-TROYTT, ESQ.,
14 BERKELEY SQUARE, LONDON, W.

Carl Magritte,
Lampe Str. 54,
Munchen,
Germany

17 August, 1889

Dear Magritte,

Very well – it shall be as you say. Although I am still unsure about the substitution of Hoffguard for Lendelson.

I spoke with Gatter yesterday. He did not send his best wishes. In fact he was abusive about you and his remarks inflammatory. I shall not reveal the extent of his calumnies here lest you become insulted or dispirited. I suspect that he was inebriated as there was a strong, unpleasant odour apparent in his chambers, the formaldehyde notwithstanding.

When I later chastised O'Fennel for crying out in the middle of the procedure he retorted: 'God is in the detail!' This meant nothing to me. Indeed I am still confused by it. Does it mean anything to you?

Yours,
Selman-Troytt

Post Script: The blade can be sharpened upon a leather strop. My butler does the same with the razor prior to shaving me. A cleft palate is always a challenge.

J. SELMAN-TROYTT, ESQ.,
14 BERKELEY SQUARE, LONDON, W.

Professor Miles Stanleyson,*
Kotherschaft Institute,
Geneva,
Switzerland

19 February, 1890

Dear Sir,

Please find enclosed some flakes of skin from the calves of my legs. *All* enclosed samples have been collected (under laboratory conditions and always in the presence of an impartial observer) from the insides of my socks.

Among the many questions such occurrences beg is the principal one I wish to lay before you: if my skin is flaking, and therefore *thinning* itself . . . then why is it still thick?

I write to you on the advice of Professor Herbert Montague – who could offer no answers but is familiar with your research on lotions.

Awaiting your advises I remain,

Your most obedient servant,
J. Selman-Troytt

* See p.29 for a short biography of the eminent lotion specialist.

Journal Notes for July 20th, 1890

Very embarrassing incident at the Athenaeum* last night. Millais** was again taunting Ruskin† publicly, having fun at his expense in front of a group of cronies who laughed behind their hands, and finally Ruskin attacked him with a bottle (which broke on Millais' temple and gashed his ear).

While Millais cradled his injured head in the centre of the dining area, Ruskin had to be restrained by three stewards who pinned him down as he screamed yet again that he was 'never impotent in the 1850s'. His violence is excusable for Millais makes the same gratuitous accusation every single time he sees Ruskin in public. I myself have heard him remark upon Ruskin's 'softness' on more than twenty occasions! Even last night, while Ruskin struggled helplessly in the hands of the stewards, Millais jeered at him and preened himself in a most embarrassing manner; and then, as a further taunt, cupped his own genitals suggestively and made several unwholesome references to 'Effie's needs'.‡ Ruskin became

---

* The Athenaeum – a Gentleman's Club in Pall Mall, London.

** Sir John Everett Millais (1829–1896). British painter and illustrator. One of founders of the Pre-Raphaelite Brotherhood. Millais was boastful of his talents and inordinately proud of his penile girth.

† John Ruskin (1819–1900). Prominent author, poet, artist and art critic.

‡ Euphemia ('Effie') Chalmers Gray (1828–1897). Effie was married to John Ruskin from 1848 until 1855, when their marriage was annulled for non-consummation. Shortly after, Effie married John Everett Millais (a protégé of John Ruskin) with whom she had already fallen in love during her marriage to Ruskin. She bore him eight children. Until her death she maintained that Millais' penile girth was such that she was 'unable to encompass it in both hands'. She was rumoured to be the author of the popular 19th century honeymoon doggerel: 'Long and thin / Slips straight in / But it's fat and thick / That does the trick', a rumour supported by her inscription of the verse on the flyleaf of the bible she presented to Millais on his death bed.

almost apoplectic once again and could not be calmed. Eventually, he had to be carried bodily from the building. Sickkersby twice asked Millais to 'Draw it mild!' but was ignored. It was a very unpleasant night. I shall never buy a work of his now.

Journal notes for July 21st, 1890

Still troubled by last night. I have been considering Ruskin's alleged condition. If Millais' accusations are true, and he has 'softness' in his parts, then I wonder if this is something that may be a fertile area for study? Could I bring my observational powers to bear on the problems of size and rigidity?* Perhaps later, when the retractor is fully realised?

Journal notes for August 3rd, 1890

Father very angry with me today. No explanation provided.

Post has arrived. Still no letter from Stanleyson with the response I am eagerly awaiting.

Have acquired several mice. May experiment upon them if suitable purpose presents itself.

* See pp.158-165 for an extended description of Selman-Troytt's attempts to cure Lord Soames's erectile dysfunction.

J. SELMAN-TROYTT, ESQ.,
14 BERKELEY SQUARE, LONDON, W.

Colonel Edgar Mullet,
Mullet Towers,
Uckfield,
Sussex

2 February, 1891

Sir!

I am outraged at your suggestion! I cannot countenance the proposition that I return any portion of your fee. Such a suggestion is insulting, as well as detrimental to my financial position!

Indeed, I should most grateful if you would deign to share with me your proposal as to how such a proportion could even be calculated in circumstances such as these. Do you intend to propose that because your wife can manage to sit for only half of her usual time then half should be retained? Ridiculous!

I tell you, Sir, that you anger me beyond measure. It will be a sorry day for all if I receive another of your hypocritical and craven importunings.

Yours &c.
Selman-Troytt

The First Time I Soiled My Trousers

A Literary Fragment

BY

JEREMY SELMAN-TROYTT

O'Rourke & LeFevre
London
MDCCCXCII

PART I

AN UNEASY FEELING

CHAPTER ONE

A Gut Reaction

In which the author
suffers a discombobulation

IN ORDER FOR THE READER to appreciate fully the circumstances in which I first soiled my trousers it will be necessary for me describe them, and also the various contributory factors which culminated in the involuntary evacuation of my bowels in a public arena, in some detail. I must therefore crave the reader's indulgence in allowing me to begin my account precisely thirteen-and-one-half minutes before the actual event.

I had been dining with some old acquaintances who chanced to be in London prior to travelling north for the 'Glorious Twelfth'. We had made a good repast at my club in Pall Mall, where my friend Jefferson Lemurre* had distinguished himself by consuming nineteen quails' eggs and an entire piglet.

Whilst the others had eaten well, but not lavishly, I had consumed but a fraction of my normal intake. My limited appetite had little to do with the quality of the fare (which was excellent) nor the conversation of my companions (which was sparkling) but was connected to an inexplicable uneasiness that I was experiencing in the pit of my stomach. For reasons which are now beyond my comprehension, I consciously forced these considerations aside in favour of observing the physical condition of those individuals assembled.

Guscott**, often an enigma, was substantially larger than only a week previously, and Quadrant had a facial swelling I did not like. It commenced about one inch to the left of his mouth and continued in a straight line, almost as a band, to the back of his neck. I calculated its protrusion at one-and-a-half inches and its width at two. He had covered it completely with a mustard plaster, ostensibly to alleviate the condition through the drawing effect of a poultice but also, I am sure, to disguise it from casual view.

In this I believe he failed, as the weight of the plaster served to unbalance his head and send his eye-line on a tilt that could be noticed by all present – however, no one was sufficiently ill-mannered as to stare or make mention of this fault.

Lenoir†, who was always accompanied by his personal physician, had retired for a fresh dressing a short time before so we were none of us discomposed by his presence. Indeed, we welcomed him back with a joviality that was no less warm for being forced.

Cartwright‡ appeared to any casual observer as his usual light-hearted self, but a closer examination revealed some seepage which he was at pains to conceal by distracting the attention of onlookers with a stream of verbal wizardry and demonstrations of *legerdemain* which filled us with wonder.

---

* See p.146

** See p.27

† See p.28

‡ See p.99

His ability to speak non-stop is a talent which I have never possessed and of which I have often felt the lack; indeed, upon occasion I have passed through periods of such appalling reticence that I have had to instruct my butler to speak on my behalf. How often have I longed, during such involuntary silences, to be the master of such verbal dexterity as that with which Cartwright dazzled us for five hours together!

But I anticipate. The time by my pocket-watch was exactly twenty-seven minutes past eight when Hemmings proffered the suggestion that we should all take a break between courses in order to allow Mainwaring to entertain us by blowing forcefully through

(Seven hundred and eighty pages here omitted. Ed.*)*

as with a gushing sensation, accompanied by a sudden rush of heat to the rim of the anus, I felt my trousers filling with a hideous and uneasy cargo that was more liquid than solid. An instinctive glance at my time-piece showed that it wanted thirty seconds of twenty-eight minutes to nine, a fact I felt compelled to record in case it should prove useful. I would have preferred to make a written notation, but having no paper to hand I was forced instead to memorise the time by chanting the numbers aloud several times in rapid succession. With these priorities completed I felt more able to direct my attention to my circumstances.

No words can describe the disgust that seized me at that instant, accompanied as it was by the realisation that my undergarments were now united with my buttocks by virtue of the sticky ordure which conjoined them. I began to shudder and pulsate, and would have fainted altogether had I not been conscious of the puzzled stares of those around me, and frightened lest they should rush to loosen my clothing upon seeing me swoon. Indeed, it was my concern for the good opinion of my companions that now overshadowed my squelching discomfiture and became my principle consideration. However, here I must halt my narrative.

IN THE FOREGOING PAGES I have done my best to summarise the practical circumstances of this soiling with candour, but also with the brevity necessary to any written account which intends to inform but not to tire. Accordingly, I have decided to halt my narrative at the actual point of the soiling. I intend dealing with all ancillary subjects – such as the extent of my immediate embarrassment and my fear lest the revolting aromas arising from my breeches should become apparent to my friends before I was able to effect an escape from the close confines of the room – in a companion work to be published in due course. Enquiries regarding this work should be directed to my publishers or their agents.

J.S-T. 1892

Contemporaries

Arthur Henry Guscott

Arthur Henry Guscott, photographed before the inflation that saw his weight balloon to 56 stones (356kg).

Before the age of twenty-one Guscott had already established something of a 'fast' reputation among the young bucks of Victorian society (he was the first man ever to be arrested for discharging a shotgun *inside* a pair of trousers) but was difficult to know and unpredictable in behaviour. He was capable of contradicting anyone, on any subject, at any time.

He had a particular penchant for strong-willed, lantern-jawed women* who exceeded him in height and weight; a desire more easily fulfilled in his early days when he stood at 5' 6" (1.67m) and weighed only 8st 5lb (53kg).

Contemporary accounts suggest that Guscott suffered from feelings of inferiority, although he always denied it vehemently and abused anyone who accused him of it. He made a point of telling all new acquaintances that he suffered from *hypertrophy*** and used a variety of means to aid the illusion. Careful study of his left inner thigh on the attached photo will show that he is wearing one of his famed 'pronouncers', possibly one from a special set carved for him from narwhal tusk by a Malay acquaintance.

---

* See p.167 for an example of this type of female.

** However a post-mortem examination showed that this was not the case.

Contemporaries

Jules and Matilde Lenoir

Connected to the famous Perpignan Lenoirs, Jules and his delightful bride came often to England for hospitalisation, preferring the then prevailing hygiene standards of the British institutions to what they described as the '*excremental filth*' of their native French clinics.

Invariably segregated in single-sex and non-adjacent establishments, the Lenoirs spent only three months together during their first eleven years of marriage.

Always loyal, Matilde once confided to a friend that she loved Jules even when he seeped '*without surcease*'.

Contemporaries

Professor Miles Stanleyson

One of Selman-Troytt's greatest inspirations, Professor Stanleyson of Geneva, the world-renowned authority on lotions, was the man to whom he sent almost three kilograms of his own shedded skin over a hectic twenty-five year correspondence. Unfortunately, owing to other commitments Stanleyson was unable ever to reply.

Stanleyson, described by colleagues as a 'fanatical obsessive', pursued his own researches remorselessly from early childhood. By his own admission he became impossible to live with after his fifth birthday.

At the age of only nine he became intrigued by the possibility of reshaping the growing body. Having only his own to work with, he constructed a funnel-shaped sleeping harness and for the next six years spent every night with his head and shoulders encased in it. "*I am interested to see if I will become shaped like a pencil*," the curious boy confided to his journal. Although he later abandoned the experiment, dismissing it as "*childish lunacy on an unprecedented scale . . . a total waste of time which has harmed my chances in the javelin*", its effects upon his upper torso are still apparent in this photograph taken almost fifty years later.

From the age of nineteen he devoted himself exclusively to the study of non-lanolin-based lotions.

Journal notes for September 4th, 1892

Many more letters arrived again today, also connected with publication of *FTISMT**. I have not had such a response to any publication before. Many of the letters were flattering and fulsome in their praise of both the writing style and the structure. Both compliments I found pleasing because they hasten my hope that those who read my work will comprehend its moral purpose without being simply overwhelmed by the scientific technicalities. One letter contained a threat to have me killed, but I assume this to be the work of someone unstable. I am not overly concerned, for I seldom venture out of doors. As a precaution though, I may send Simpkins abroad as a decoy, dressed in my frock coat and hat to establish whether an assailant can be drawn into the open and his identity revealed in the process. I will instruct Simpkins to memorise the features of anyone who attacks him.

Journal notes for September 7th, 1892

Three journalists called today at different times, seeking to discuss the popularity of *FTISMT,* but I had Fairbanks dismiss them immediately for they were low, vulgar types with sideburns. How dare they disturb my work with these intolerable interruptions! I am a man of science, not a society raconteur or a performing bear!

Journal notes for September 8th, 1892

More callers! I will not have my work disturbed in such a manner.

---

* *The First Time I Soiled My Trousers*, O'Rourke & LeFevre: London, 1892

JOURNAL NOTES FOR JULY 27TH, 1893

Another restless night, apparently. My third since records began*. But I have no explanation save the possibility that I am disturbed by contemplation of my work. I am haunted constantly by the premonition of a startling breakthrough.

Am angered beyond measure to discover that my trousers, which were sent to my tailor for lengthening, have been returned with the fly closed.

Lunch short – soup strange but not unpleasant. Avocados producing no noticeable effect. Have issued each member of staff with 5lbs of lentils and strict instructions.

NOTE: I discover by measurement that the circumference of my thigh ($19\frac{3}{8}$ inches) is very similar to that of my ankle ($17\frac{7}{8}$ inches), and that they are in the ratio $1{:}\,1^{12}/_{143}$. . . Significant? Connection with other ratios? E.g. neck to bicep, wrist to waist, etc.? Could such correlation be related to wealth, as with phrenology? Must pursue. Measure staff tomorrow.

JOURNAL NOTES FOR JUNE 9TH, 1894

All frogs now twice normal size. Newts unchanged. An anomaly. I am both angered and unsettled. Interestingly, nothing happened to

* Brief details of this recording procedure can be found on pp.74-75 in *My First Nocturnal Emission*. A more comprehensive account can be found in *Patterns of Sleep – 9,000 Detailed Observations Made Minute by Minute*. Both by Jeremy Selman-Troytt and published by O'Rourke & LeFevre, London.

the newts even when I brushed on the third application of silver nitrate. This is a frustration I could have done without in my present physical state.

Richards writes to say that he prospers, and that his family are well, and that he wishes me well. Why does he bother me with this trivia at such a critical stage?

Journal notes for August 27th, 1894

Very hot and difficult evening with Dundry in Athenaeum. Between six o'clock and ten minutes of nine he maintained persistently and argumentatively that he had erectile dysfunction, and when those assembled there cast doubts upon the notion he then angrily displayed a rigidly erect penis to prove his point! I, for one, was infuriated. When I pointed out the self-evident contradiction he became inflamed and abusive. Gatter, Cholpley and Sturge sided with me, but Guscott supported Dundry (again!) – I suspect out of contrariness. I think it made me realise how much I hate Guscott, even though he has been a close friend for many years.

I took my leave within minutes to signal my displeasure, and walked home with my thighs chafing painfully.

J. SELMAN-TROYTT, ESQ.,
14 BERKELEY SQUARE, LONDON, W.

Ernest Moffat,
Butcher and Poulterer,
Keynsham Lane,
London, E.

30 August, 1894

Moffat,

My butler tells me that although he has insisted repeatedly upon an improvement in the quality of goods you supply, we have again received a consignment of fatty meat.

I tell you again, Sir: I do not like fat! I will not have it near me. It promotes mental torpor and furnishes no nourishment nor purpose save to add itself with enthusiasm to those already obese. Save your fat for other people! I will not have it in my house.

If your next delivery is not all lean then I shall box the ears of your delivery boy.

Selman-Troytt

J. Selman-Troytt, Esq.,
14 Berkeley Square, London, W.

Miss S. Fowles,
13 Mincing Lane,
London, E.

11 September, 1894

Madam,

If you are getting no relief then I would suggest a double application. Or even a triple. In fact, I would apply the ointment continually until either relief were obtained or the jar emptied. In the latter case you will need to replenish your supply and fresh ointment can be purchased from me at a cost of £1.3s.6d for a small jar, or 5 guineas for a large one. I realise that it is expensive, but this is because it is the only preparation that can bring you relief and this, of course, affects the price at which I decide to sell it to you.

As demonstrated to you in my surgery, the ointment should be applied with a circular rubbing motion, although not strongly enough to abrade the skin or strain the arm muscles. And it should be applied liberally, even lavishly.

Your most humble and obedient servant,
J. Selman-Troytt

The First Time I Soiled My Trousers

Volume II

BY

JEREMY SELMAN-TROYTT

O'Rourke & LeFevre
London
MDCCCXCIV

PART I

A DESPERATE SITUATION

CHAPTER ONE

I Am Embarrassed

In which the author becomes embarrassed by prevailing circumstances

IN THE PRIMARY PART OF this account I dealt with the circumstances in which I first soiled my trousers, but owing to the constraints of writing within a 'readable' length of manuscript – that is, one which can be read by any normal reader within seven days, allowing two uninterrupted hours per day for that pursuit – whilst at the same time preserving to the fore of my mind an acute consciousness of the necessity to sustain a writing style that would at once entice and beguile but never fatigue, I was in that account able to deal only with the practical circumstances of the soiling during the antecedent period *immediately* prior to the evacuation.

Subsequent pertinent factors – such as my embarrassment that such an unheralded and disturbing catastrophe should explode into my otherwise calm existence, or my worry lest my friends should become aware of my revolting condition, or my fears that my efforts to escape their presence unexposed should fail – had to be omitted and I was, on that consideration, compelled to suffer the frustration of recounting only one part (indeed I described it, with no little justification, as a 'fragment') of a situation which must needs display all its facets in order for the reader to have understood the whole in anything approaching an accurate assessment.

My frustration is in part mitigated now by my opportunity to deal with those other facets here, but I beg any reader of this volume who has not already studied the former work to cease this perusal immediately and to proceed through both volumes in chronological sequence lest he obtain but a partial glimpse of this extraordinary episode.

My state of mind upon becoming cognizant of my condition is one that may only be conjectured by those who have yet to suffer a similar ordeal: it was one in which disgust, incredulity, fear, reserve, repugnance, abhorrence, displeasure, concern, discomfort, and extreme nervous debility all jostled for supremacy in their attempt to unseat my reason. Indeed, my efforts to maintain my *sang-froid* notwithstanding, I have little doubt that my features betrayed something of the maelstrom that raged beneath, for several of my companions enquired as to the palatability of the course I was then engaged in consuming.

I replied to the best of my ability, although no doubt in a distracted fashion – I have no recollection now of whether or not I commended the dish and did not think to make a note of my verdict at the time – for the foremost thought that began to echo and resound throughout this emotional discombobulation concerned the ardent hope that the close weave of my thick serge breeches might serve as a type of barrier that would be impermeable to both the aroma and the waste itself. But even as I conceived this thought I was forced to abandon it in desperation. I am far from pessimistic in outlook, maintaining always a positive cast of thought regarding the outcome of events, but my former experiences in the experimental sciences informed me that it was but a question of time before the contents of my trousers leached through the substantial, but nevertheless permeable, serge. At once I conjectured how different it might be if my undergarments were made of oilskin, or some other impervious material such as *caoutchouc*-impregnated canvas, and with both leg sections tightened close to my thighs with leather straps. I resolved to reserve the thought for future consideration and study, and make mention of it here to illustrate how the minds of those who are drawn towards scientific study by virtue of their disposition, temperament, or leaning can never be wholly distracted from that pursuit.

I should say here that it was obvious to me from the start that I had to depart immediately and I began making preparations for my leave-taking, determining that I would take the first opportunity

(Five hundred and twenty-one pages here omitted. Ed.*)*

but seeing himself pursued he reversed direction, climbed back down the ladder and placed the salmon mousse on a high shelf. We all laughed gustily. Cadwallader, in celebration, determined to singe the hairs from the boar's skin in order to produce first-rate crackling. In that moment I seized my opportunity. Rising *very* slowly, and without any sudden movement that might attract attention, so that it took a full four minutes for me to attain an upright posture, I then began moving sideways, crab-like, towards the door.

The self-loathing and disgust which I experienced with every touch of my clothing threatened to overwhelm me, but was superseded by a desire to obtain my freedom undetected. By dint of such subtle and unobtrusive movements I reached the door in a little under seven minutes (fortunately, my predicament notwithstanding, my sense of duty asserted itself and I had the presence of mind not only to time my movements but also to make notes upon my shirt cuff).

My hand was but six inches from the door latch when I was arrested by a shout from one of my companions. I froze in place and then turned in dread at the prospect of exposure, but was initially relieved, and then heartily pleased, to discover that the object of their attention was another of our party, one Senor Rodolpho Brazin*, who was suffering a kind of fit (either of apoplexy or pulmonary collapse) and had subsided onto his plate. Uttering a silent prayer to Our Lord for this timely distraction, I pulled open the door and fled into the darkened streets of St. James's and thence, by a judiciously selected series of back-alleys and side-streets, to my London address and the refreshing and very welcome ministrations of my butler.

I declare that this is a true and accurate account of events that night and further that, although I did not at the time consider the prudence of preserving the soiled trousers as evidence (henceforth I shall allow no such oversight), I can provide testimony from my manservant who cleaned me and is willing to swear an affidavit as to my condition.

J. S-T. 1894

* See p.96

Journal notes for 8th February, 1895

Several disturbing letters published in the correspondence section of *The Times* today. My name was alluded to in a violent debate between correspondents. I find that it makes me uncomfortable to be discussed by others. It is an unpleasant experience, for I am a very private man and prefer to keep the intimate details of my private life within my own purview.

More letters in our domestic postal delivery, although none from Stanleyson. I shall write to him again after dinner. One letter was from Oscar Wilde and was supportive and complimentary.

J. Selman-Troytt, Esq.,
14 Berkeley Square, London, W.

Mr. Oscar Wilde,
16 Tite Street,
Chelsea,
London, W.

9 February, 1895

Dear Mr. Wilde,

I thank you for your letter with its enclosed cutting of your review published in *The Times* on Tuesday last. Your comments about my latest work were an unexpected kindness, and were no less welcome for being unsolicited. I fear my work must seem dry and uninspiring next to your own, for I am a man of science and not a pederast.

I thank you also for the flowers and chocolates that arrived this morning. They are most gracious gifts, although I cannot identify the flowers because I know nothing of flora, having devoted myself to a lifelong study of human anatomy.

Your invitation that I should spend a weekend in the country with you and Lord Alfred Douglas is one that I fear I must decline, for I seldom leave the house without pressing reason and find speaking aloud in company a trying experience. Also I cannot swim, having never learned, and therefore do not own the bathing costume you requested I bring.

Your most obedient servant,
J. Selman-Troytt

Journal notes for 9th September, 1895

Simpkins injured today during initial trial of new cantilever. Scrotum torn.

Journal notes for 1st May, 1896

Meeting with Hoffmann and Fulton. Hoffmann read us a paper he had written on the nervous system. I was a good deal bored with it, for his experiments are on newts and I am more interested in humans.* Fulton demonstrated a new invention that he claimed would discharge small amounts of electricity into the fingertips. We all tried it and found that it performed exactly as he forecast. Fulton is now looking for a practical application for the apparatus so that he can apply for a patent.

* This preference notwithstanding, Selman-Troytt did on occasion use newts to illuminate his ideas. See for example p.199.

Family

The Aunts

Very little is documented about either of Jeremy's maiden aunts, Jennifer (left) and Jacobina (below), beyond their much vaunted chastity. We know that Jennifer was rather reticent, speaking only eleven words between 1864 and 1879, while her sister spoke non-stop, even whilst breathing in.

Both seem to have encouraged Jeremy in his scientific studies. Jacobina defended him more than once to his openly contemptuous father, whilst one letter from a seventeen-year-old Jeremy begins: '*Dear Aunt Jennifer, I write to express my gratitude to you for allowing me to examine your rampant desquamation. It was an astounding experience which I cannot forget. When I am older I shall describe it to Stanleyson in Geneva and request that he find you an appropriate lotion . . .*'

Family

Jolyon Selman-Troytt

A noted *dilettante* and *bon viveur*, Jeremy's older brother Jolyon (left, seated right) spent a lot of time having his jacket sponged clean. He was a frequent visitor to the house of Oscar Wilde, but was always refused admittance on the grounds that he was not known there.

His very public marriage to the energetic and beautiful Doña Yolanda Cortez (below), a match engineered by his father Josiah and remarkable for the presence of a dozen Lipizzaner horses inside the wedding chapel, was the talk of Victorian society. As Yolanda swept up the aisle, the train of her dress stretched a full fifty metres behind her, along the aisle, over the occasional mound of fresh droppings, and out into the sunlight that bathed the adoring crowds who waited in eager anticipation of kissing an unstained part of it.

The Doña was often described as the woman with the '*most tempting Spanish eyes in London*', and Gladstone was moved to say that '*her luscious curves would make even a clergyman consider coition with a woman*'.

Ruskin wrote of her: '*She bathes me in filmy perspiration at the very thought of her taut musculature and pouting, firm breasts*', while Dante Rossetti was so obsessed with her that he painted her in four very explicit 'erotic' poses where she lay sinuously draped around a male partner who was stimulating her manually to the point of orgasm. The male partner was Rossetti himself, and in these self-portraits he worked with a mirror above the bed, his free hand holding a paint brush up to a canvas positioned directly above the head-board.

However, despite her abundant physical charms it is not clear whether her marriage to Jolyon was ever consummated. Jolyon spent most of his spare time at the home of Douglas Hearne (above left, seated left) a railway booking clerk and amateur apiarist. Little is known about the relationship beyond some entries in Jolyon's journal in which he records that he '*spent many a wonderful afternoon mounting bees*' in the back parlour of Hearne's modest south London house in Norwood.

Journal notes for 21st July, 1896

Reflecting today on the ways in which my life has become enriched and more satisfying since I began attempting to design a portable version of the prepuce retractor.

A minor accident in the laboratory this afternoon. Misjudged distance and struck ball of right eye on the eyepiece of microscope. Enormously painful. Bathed it in witch-hazel and applied poultice. Tonight I am monocular.

Stanleyson not yet replied. I shall write to him again tomorrow.

Sometimes I feel the great weight of public expectation upon my shoulders.

PART TWO

The Romance Years

1897–1908

Journal notes for January 11th, 1897

A breakthrough idea! Hugely important! One that may prove a milestone. Since embarking upon the challenge of making the retractor portable some twelve years ago, I have concentrated my efforts exclusively on making the apparatus small enough to be packed into a suitcase of medium size. However, as I sat in my work room tonight, I had an immense afflatus!

For the first time, I was struck by the thought that one need not limit one's efforts to a suitcase! I began to consider a host of other ideas – the retractor could be carried by a servant, perhaps, or drawn upon a small cart. Or it could even be contained within a case carried upon the back in the manner of a knapsack. The ideas were many and passed through my mind with frightening rapidity.

Many ideas were of no value ultimately, but from the white heat of that alchemy I plucked an idea so exciting, so audacious, that I find myself trembling slightly as I write this – for it will allow even the poor to retract their prepuces, so that class need not be a barrier to hygiene!

The new retractor is to be *back mounted*, a radical alteration to the design that will at once remove some weight concerns as well as the need for an expensive leather case. I have made a preliminary sketch* to record the basic idea on paper before the details unravel and I become lost in the welter of complexity that can overwhelm one occasionally. The illustration should prove sufficient as a basis for Jennings & Evincourt to work up some technical drawings for a prototype.

---

* See Appendix III(c) p.247.

I am so excited! Sleep will evade me tonight as a certainty. Perhaps I shall sit and try to talk with Simpkins, although I am not sure that I am equal to the challenge since the poor boy is an uneducated and uninformed oaf with very limited intellect.

JOURNAL NOTES FOR MAY 27TH, 1897

Another breakthrough idea! Although my efforts to date have been concentrated towards weight reduction in order to make the retractor portable, it has long been at the back of my mind that another problem will require to be overcome eventually, to wit: *how to introduce the retractor safely to the organ*. The problem is thus: if the organ is taken out manually and introduced to the retractor then the hands have already been contaminated, which renders the retractor wholly pointless. Conversely, if the prepuce clamp is inserted directly through the trouser fly in the hope of locating the organ then one is groping blindly and could easily damage a testicle.

So far I have regarded this problem as of secondary importance, since obviously one must first resolve the problem of constructing the retractor before the issue of access to the prepuce even arises. However, today a solution came to me in a blinding flash whilst I was eating a toasted scone. I realised that there was a third way! Instead of bringing the organ out, or thrusting the retractor in, I conceived of a way in which the glans could be exposed without contact from human hand! It is an idea so simple and elegant in design that I am berating myself for not having conceived of it before, especially when the solution lay before me all the time. The answer is the trouser fly itself!

In its present design the fly is both blessing and curse: a blessing insofar as it allows the wearer to micturate outside his trousers; a curse insofar as it necessitates reaching into a confined and unsettling space in order to make contact with oneself in a way that is wholly unsanitary.

I had earlier toyed briefly with the idea of lengthening or widening the trouser fly, but the problem of reaching inside was not satisfactorily solved by either method. However, today I realised that the solution lay not in extension, but rather in multiplication! In simple terms, another fly introduced at the back of the trousers, as well as one at either side, will enable all four sections of the upper trousers to be loosened and then peeled downwards, not unlike a banana. This will enable one to expose one's organ without bringing one's hands within three inches of it!

I am very excited indeed! I shall send to Cardews with a design in the morning and have them tailor a product prototype for me. It is at moments like these that I realise that one's labours, if they are at times challenging, are also a wondrous bounty!

Journal notes for June 1st, 1897

Intrigued by Warburton's collapse at Ascot. Nostril closure? Size? Shape? Alternate explanation? Blockage in trachea? Could he have inhaled a strawberry?

Journal notes for June 4th, 1897

Should Scudder be that moist? Typically Hanson disagrees with me and says: 'Yes'. This is absurd. What right has he to contradict me when he is no more than a dilettante? Effusions need to be drawn, whether by poultice or hot cup, in order to create the dryness necessary to promote healing by secondary intention. By my reckoning, Scudder should have been dry on March 3rd.

Journal notes for June 8th, 1897

Wrote to Stanleyson, complete with skin samples.

Journal notes for June 11th, 1897

Multiple-fly trousers arrived today from tailor and they are an unequivocal success! I am so pleased, for it is not often that one strikes absolutely the correct note first time.

As soon as the tailor's boy left I bade Fairbanks dress me in the trousers. He was able to master them on the first attempt by carefully following my instructions, and when they were fitted I turned this way and that in the looking glass and could see absolutely no indication of the presence of additional flies. For all the world they looked like a normal pair of trousers. Yet I was then able to stand before the mirror, and by dint of unbuttoning each fly with my fingertips only, slowly peel down each trouser quadrant to fully expose my genitals and buttocks without once bringing my hands closer than two inches to any offensive areas. Fairbanks was astounded, and simply could not believe his eyes when he saw the trouser quadrants peel back as if by sorcery. Again and again he shook his head in bewilderment. I laughed at his discombobulation but then determined to put him out of his misery by demonstrating how I had managed it. Even then, it required three repetitions before he began to grasp the fundamentals of what was happening. Again, I was moved to chuckle at his complete disorientation, for the complexity of the trousers is far beyond the comprehension of a layman.

I can now return to the crucial work of lightening the prepuce retractor, knowing that the problem of access is solved. Excellent! I am sure I shall sleep like a baby tonight! Really bucked!

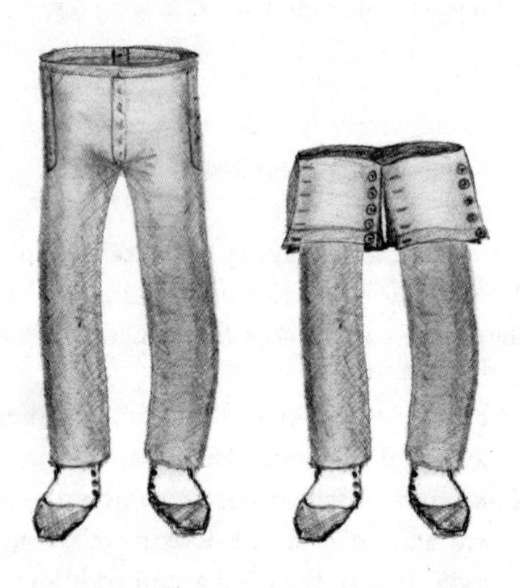

Aubrey Beardsley's impression of the multiple-fly trousers during a demonstration before Edward, Prince of Wales at Balmoral Castle, Scotland. (This is Beardsley's last known work before his death in 1898.)

JOURNAL NOTES FOR JUNE 20TH, 1897

An amusing incident this morning. Upon arising I bade Simpkins dress me in the new multiple-fly trousers. He had not seen them before and therefore had no idea what lay in store. He assumed them to be perfectly normal trousers and I gave no indication in any other wise. I simply stood stock still and watched in amusement as he attempted to comprehend them, holding them up first one way and then the other, then turning them around and around in his hands. Their construction was a complete mystery to him. I watched the poor fellow's face as he struggled with the confusion of finding more than one fly. I fancy he may have been able to cope with two, but the third and fourth overwhelmed him completely. Finally he just stood awkwardly, holding the trousers and gaping at me, events before him having moved at a speed that was simply too fast for his brain to process. Finally, I took pity on him and allowed him to lie on his cot for an hour or two to collect his senses. Although I meant nothing malicious, I did enjoy watching his astonishment, feeling an additional fillip for knowing that I was wholly responsible for the advanced design that had amazed him so.

Later in the day, when he was himself once more, I demonstrated the trousers to him. I did it slowly and deliberately, but still he shook his head continually, not sure that he could believe the evidence of his own eyes as my genitals appeared as though by magic.

Journal notes for August 5th, 1897

I have shaved a guinea pig with the intention of testing lotions upon it. I am considering a less caustic variety of the compound that caused the excessive scaliness on Marjoribanks.

Family

Joan & 'The Twins'

Although none of Josiah's daughters was ever allowed a role in the family business, they indulged in various machinations in the domestic sphere. For example, Joan (left) was terrorised by 'The Twins' (below) who threatened to murder her with a bread knife if she ever dressed in anything other than black. 'The Twins', by contrast, dressed exclusively in white, and always alike.

More sinister yet is that 'The Twins' were not actually twins at all! Born Jane and Jacinth, but *thirteen months* apart, they lived a normal childhood existence until the ages of four and five respectively, at which time they declared themselves to be twins and could not be shaken from this conviction even by Josiah's violence. Right up to the very end of their lives* they lived, slept, prayed, and ate together wearing identical outfits.

* A suicide pact at the age of 74 and 75.

Family

Joseph and Mary Selman-Troytt

From the moment he met Mary Splint-Parquet, Jeremy's elder brother Joseph decided that fate had provided him with an opportunity that was too good to miss. Their name combination appealed immediately to his ironic sense of humour, and as soon as she accepted his marriage proposal he began to make plans that their first-born would be called Jesus, even if it were a girl.

Life held several cruel disappointments for Jesus (below right). He never was selected for the school nativity play despite repeated auditions well into his late teens, and he also failed in his other ambition of being accepted for study at Jesus College, Cambridge (he longed for the opportunity to spread mirth and make friends by greeting other undergraduates with '*Hello, I'm Jesus at Jesus*'). He made a second unsuccessful entry attempt the following year, and when he was rejected also by Jesus College, Oxford he lost interest in the idea of further education and forewent university altogether.

Unable to cope with continuing disappointment, he withdrew into himself and eventually faded into obscurity, rarely leaving the house. None of the family could recall seeing him after 1906.

Family

Jeffrey Selman-Troytt

Nowadays Jeffrey might be described as having 'Munchausen's Syndrome', but in the latter part of the nineteenth century he was simply one of a significant minority of Englishmen who insisted upon an annual haemorrhoidectomy whether they had haemorrhoids or not. For them it was part of a set ritual, like shaving body hair or attending church.

Jeremy found Jeffrey's repeated visits increasingly annoying, and shortly prior to a fourth operation he attempted to demur, declaring that the procedure was '*unnecessary, as there is nothing there to cut. Nothing!*' But Jeffrey sought support from the whole Selman-Troytt family, who closed ranks and insisted upon Jeffrey's right to have something removed if he wished.

Jeffrey's bicycle (a luxurious 120-guinea *Carson & Henk* with cast-iron rims and attenuated fork reducers) never left his side and was a source of enormous psychological comfort to him. He was not able actually to ride it, as very little of his rectum remained, but he insisted on pushing it around with him to suggest to passers-by that his rectum was intact.

JOURNAL NOTES FOR NOVEMBER 23RD, 1897

Another meeting with Father this morning. Without warning he bade me come into the drawing room where he was shouting at Dr Temple and Mr. Maclagan* about finances. While they sat in the room and stared at me disconcertingly, he demanded that I demonstrate progress to date in order to prove that further research monies would be a worthwhile investment.

It was a very awkward moment and I yearned to refuse. My latest lotions have yet to precipitate and construction of the retractor is still not complete (as several problems have yet to be overcome). Furthermore, I am always reticent in company, and the idea of demonstrating in public was terrifying. However, there was no alternative as I cannot continue without the funding, so I bade Fairbanks fetch the equipment while a subject was selected. Father became impatient with the process and volunteered Mr. Maclagan in spite of his age.

The demonstration was not an unqualified success. Mr. Maclagan showed reasonable dexterity with the cantilevers in spite of his advanced years, but the friction problem was still evident in the bearing surfaces and caught him unawares, causing an unexpected pressure surge that crushed his right testicle. However, Father was sufficiently impressed to allow my funding to continue. I was so pleased that I almost demonstrated the four-piece 'peel-down' trousers but reasoned that it would be prudent to keep something in reserve for our next funding meeting.

---

* Frederick Temple and William Maclagan, Archbishops of Canterbury and York respectively.

J. SELMAN-TROYTT, ESQ.,
14 BERKELEY SQUARE, LONDON, W.

Hon. Cecil Lanchester,
11 Partingham Square,
London, W.

15 December, 1897

Dear Lanchester,

With reference to your invitation of 11th *inst.*

I have considered it at great length, attempting to balance the positive elements against the negative.

On the positive side it presents an opportunity (possibly) for some mental stimulation and good sport, in addition to the obvious inducement of excellent fare at your table. I remember my last visit to your home, and am able to recall with great clarity the quality of food and wine on offer.

However, against these must be weighed the negative aspects of a visit to your house, not least among which is the need to endure company in general and your own in particular. (You know that I have had cause upon several occasions to draw to your attention those of your habits and mannerisms which I find difficult or annoying.) In addition, there is the inconvenience attendant upon dressing, leaving my house, travelling, tipping your servants, returning home, &c.

My tardiness in replying to you is a measure of how finely balanced I have found the scales to be in this instance, with no clear indication as to whether the disadvantages of attending will be outweighed by the advantages.

After much deliberation I have decided that I shall take a risk and attend. At the very least I shall be well fed. However, should it transpire that the evening is unpleasant, or is a waste of my time, or appears to present no ready justification as to why we should have been assembled in the name of entertainment, then I shall file that information away for future reference.

Therefore, expect me upon the 18th. Set a place for me at table at 8 o'clock. I will eat, although I doubt I shall speak. However, I reserve the right to change my mind upon the latter.

Yours &c.
Selman-Troytt

Journal notes for July 2nd, 1898

A wonderful inspiration struck today as I attended a friendly football match between the Camperavians (the senior's team at Guscott's old college) and the Olavians from Cheltenham. It was my first exposure to a football match and, bringing my extensive powers of observation to bear upon it, I was quick to note that running about in the hot sun had a progressively deleterious effect upon each player's performance, causing him to pant and perspire. This in turn caused each player to slow down as the match progressed, so that those who commenced the match bounding like spring hares finished it at a much more pedestrian pace. One player, quite fat to begin with, was completely stationary at the end and had to be lifted bodily and carried from the field by a large number of helpful volunteers. Guscott confided to me that Ploombs (the fat player) often ran himself into total immobility.

Observing the players' reddened faces, unsteady gait and swollen tongues, I deduced of a sudden that the problem must be connected with dehydration. Almost at once an idea came to me that may provide a solution! I am almost beside myself with excitement, but I shall pursue the matter vigorously on a cerebral level before committing more to paper.

Journal notes for July 3rd, 1898

I have now considered the matter cerebrally, turning it this way and that, and can find fault neither with the premise nor with the amazingly simple solution it presents. For if dehydration is indeed the cause of the players' diminished physical powers, then it follows that players could run indefinitely if it were able to be prevented, *because they would be unimpeded by its effects!* They would become, in effect, perpetual motion machines, able to run for years without stopping. And they could continue to run *swiftly*, with no diminution of speed. Against any team suffering normal dehydration they would be wholly unassailable.

I sense I am on the edge of a breakthrough.

Journal notes for July 4th, 1898

I find it interesting that hardened foodstuffs may be loosened from clothing more readily by softening with water.

Seed pods still fertile although casings are now leathery. Lack of lanolin?

Journal notes for July 7th, 1898

Seed pods withered!

Journal notes for July 8th, 1898

I have given nearly a week's thought to the problem of preventing dehydration in football players and believe I now have the basis for a working hypothesis.

It is clear that bodily dehydration increases as the game progresses, as evidenced by the thirst that the players display at half-time and full time. Patently, therefore, the body is using its fluids in some way – possibly to produce the perspiration that soaks constantly into the players' clothing from the instant the game commences. It seems logical to deduce that the body would prefer to replenish this moisture contemporaneously with its loss, thereby keeping the player fully moist internally at all times. Ergo, it is clearly inefficient for each player to run for a full forty-five minutes before he can replenish his bodily fluids.

Therefore, as a solution, I propose that each player carry a small water-filled bladder (perhaps worn discreetly on the upper back, under the shirt – I have not yet considered the design in detail) from which a hose will protrude. When fluid is required, the hose can simply be clamped between the teeth and sucked. Very excited by this!

I shall begin work on a prototype design this evening and have today contacted Agnew's* in Piccadilly to put them on notice that I will require some equipment manufactured to my precise specifications. Obviously the harness must be strong enough to bear the load of bladder and contents combined, yet light enough to be worn unnoticed. Or, if not altogether unnoticed, then at least it must not impede the player physically. I am considering leather

* Agnew's were responsible for making the bladders for Livingstone's Zambezi expedition in 1858.

straps with brass buckles that will not corrode. The bladder itself must, perforce, be wholly watertight.

JOURNAL NOTES FOR JULY 10TH, 1898

Excellent progress! Finished a prototype design (cross-shoulder pattern) with which the experiment can be started, and have sent it to Agnew's for them to produce. They promise delivery within one week. Today I received a letter from the coach of the Camperavians, granting his cooperation in the experiment. For my first trial I shall equip half the team with bladders, with the other half acting as a comparison. If my expectations are met, the bladder wearers will maintain better fitness, maintain more consistent speeds, and be less adversely affected by the physical demands of running in hot weather.

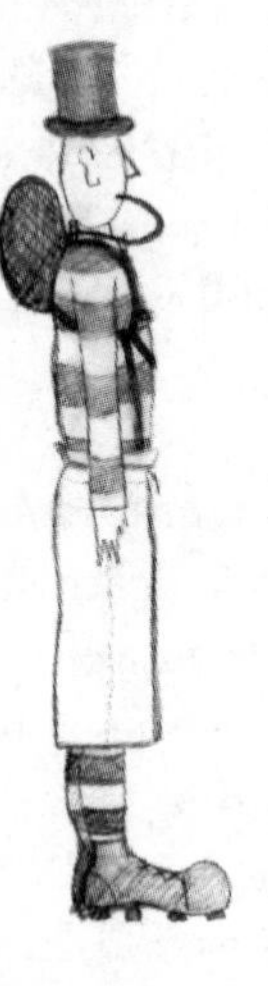

If I am correct, such an astounding scientific breakthrough may prompt colleagues to suggest that I be given some sort of accolade, such as a knighthood or a seat at the Royal Society, for my services to humanity. Of course I shall refuse any such ostentatious and embarrassing tribute at once, for I care not for any personal acclaim or advancement but seek merely to add to the march of technical progress. What true man of science could want more?

Still no response from Stanleyson. I checked the letter tray twice.

JOURNAL NOTES FOR JULY 15TH, 1898

Noted today that all members of staff have different body weights.

For example, Fairbanks weighs more than Grafton, even though both are men. Discrepancies between men and women may perhaps be more easily accepted, but between people of the same gender it seems curious. I shall consider whether something might be done to Fairbanks and Grafton to equalise their weight.

Post Script: I have today noticed that my left thigh is now twice the circumference of my right. I have initiated hourly observations.

Journal notes for July 17th, 1898

The bladders have arrived! A very exciting day. Fairbanks filled one upon my instructions and strapped it on Simpkins' shoulders. The poor fellow almost buckled under the weight but this was to be expected as has neither the constitution nor sturdy physique of a sportsman. His body weight is only 6st 1 lb (38.6kg) The bladder was noticeable on him, even under a dress shirt; but I may be able to refine the design if the process proves successful.

I have taken note of the gross weight of a complete bladder (bladder, water and securing harness) at 30lb 7oz (13.9kg). I can scarcely wait to begin the trial, although with so much at stake I must confess to increasing trepidation.

Journal notes for July 28th, 1898

A setback, but I am not disheartened, as fortunately I was able to conceive of a solution quickly, before despair enveloped me.

Today we equipped half of the Camperavians with full bladders, leaving the remainder to play in the normal fashion without water intake.

For the first ten or fifteen minutes all went well. Although the bladder carriers took time to adapt to their higher centre of gravity (some toppling clean over on tight turns), once they had rediscovered their sense of balance they moved with alacrity despite the weights on their shoulders. They sucked frequently upon their hoses, taking in a gulp of moisture every thirty seconds, as instructed. In this regard the bladders performed faultlessly.

Those problems that did arise were due to an oversight on my part. I had hoped for a natural equilibrium within the players, insofar as liquid taken in would equal liquid expelled by the body as perspiration (excepting any small portion needed by the body for any other purposes going on within its own natural processes). In this hope I was overly optimistic, for a surplus somehow found its way into the intestinal bladders of the subjects, causing them considerable discomfort as they became painfully swollen. One player felt such desperation that he feigned injury in a tackle so that he could lie face down and micturate into the grass while pretending to recover.

It is a setback; I will not deny it. Allied with my disappointment is a sense of self-recrimination, for I feel I should have anticipated this problem. However, during half-time when several incapacitated players were being assisted to places of relief by kindly colleagues, a solution came to me that was at once as simple as it was obvious: to relieve the pressure on his intestinal bladder, it is necessary only to equip each player with an external 'overflow' bladder of some kind! The solution arrived in time to restore my confidence.

I began preliminary work on designs earlier this evening and am sure of a breakthrough.

Journal notes for July 30th, 1898

Dr Twimsatt called again (third time this month) despite knowing that I find his wife oafish and that I do not welcome his visits.

Journal notes for July 31st, 1898

Dr Twimsatt has called again!

He brought a small bag of nuts but no nutcracker. He pressed some coal tongs into service as a substitute and we three sat there in silence for almost two hours, with Mrs Twimsatt and me as mute observers whilst Twimsatt selfishly busied himself with cracking his nuts to the exclusion of everything else. Prior to departure he was at pains to ensure that each servant was given a nut. His wife was unendurable, a point I have reiterated three times to them both – once yesterday and twice today.

After he left I confiscated the nuts.

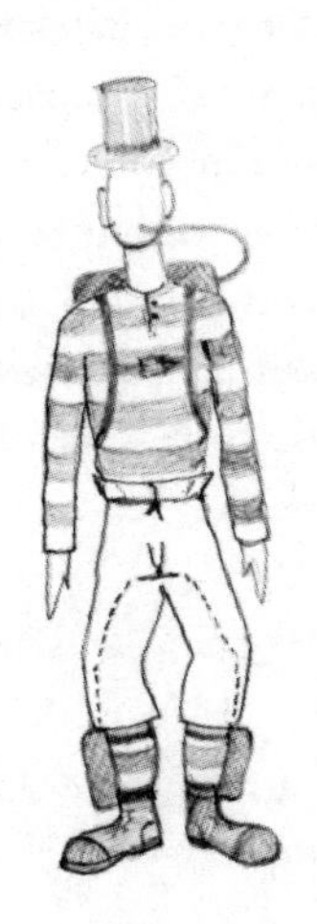

Journal notes for August 2nd, 1898

A solution! The problem can be resolved easily by catheterising each player and then equipping him with twin 'leg bladders', to which the catheter will be connected by means of rubber tubing and a connecting T-piece! In this way any liquid 'overflow' can be accommodated and allowed to accumulate gradually and continually. It is a solution at once simple and elegant.

I find that I am most tremendously bucked; my faith in living things is restored once more! I have made a preliminary sketch for Agnew's consideration and have returned to each servant the nut that I confiscated after Dr Twimsatt's departure.

Journal notes for August 5th, 1898

My good mood continues and my spirits remain high.

A messenger boy bought news from Agnew's that the 'leg bladders' will be ready in eleven days, so we should have them in time for the match against the Olavians on the 18th.

Still no response from Stanleyson.

Journal notes for August 12th, 1898

I have today encountered the word 'persiflage' and am considering whether it may be of value in romantic situations as an aid to wooing. Possibly when used in combination with other words such as 'panache'? Cholpley tells me that many ladies are amused and much influenced by language with a French flavour and that they will giggle when addressed in French. I have no French but could learn some if it were necessary to acquire a wife. It would be a worthwhile investment for the research possibilities that a conjugal union would provide.

Journal notes for August 18th, 1898

I am inconsolable and in despair! Why must I insist upon holding so close to my experiments, my hopes and dreams reaching their zenith one minute before plunging to their nadir the next?

The 'leg bladders' arrived yesterday and were found to be in perfect order. I had specified that they should be made of caoutchouc-covered canvas to keep them watertight and durable, in order to prevent them bursting under impact during heavy tackling. This necessitated a small increase in weight but I felt it was justified in the interest of security.

Having considered all eventualities, therefore, I was most optimistic about a positive conclusion. However, the following unforeseen effects were recorded:

1. Several players objected to being catheterised, and the insertion had to be carried out forcibly, thereby delaying the start of the match.
2. The match progressed as before in Trial 1, with players running easily whilst carrying their equipment; but as their 'back bladders' emptied, their 'leg bladders' filled in proportion, so that what they actually experienced was a downward transfer of weight and a lowering of their centres of gravity. Although each player was carrying only a little more weight than in the previous trial (to wit, his own body weight, plus water and various bladders – a gross weight now of 36lb 9oz) increasingly it was borne by the legs rather than the shoulders.
3. As their 'leg bladders' filled, each player became more ponderous in his movements, such that over the first thirty-five minutes of the game some players were clearly slowing: from sprinting, to loping, to jogging, to walking, and finally to a kind of stumbling gait where each leg had to be lifted clear of the ground with very obvious effort. Their movements resembled nothing so much as men trying to walk in very heavy shoes, or wade through a swamp. Consquently, the opposition team was able to dribble past them with ease and score very heavily.
4. I had neglected to consider the negative effect upon the spirits engendered by accidents. Several bladders burst during heavy body contact, causing those nearby to be showered with the contents. This

occasioned intense anger in those wetted early on and who had to complete the game in sodden jerseys they found offensive.

I feel close to despair! Almost two months of work ruined completely. I am reminded of Welkshers' recorded feelings after the failure of his work with Needlesham on the amputees at Heidelberg. I am plunged into the depths. At times such as these it is difficult not to wish myself harm.

Journal notes for August 23rd, 1898

Twice today I have found fluff on the furniture. I am concerned that this may be a form of silent rebellion over the confiscation of the nuts. Fairbanks has been ordered to convey my concerns to the other staff.

Journal notes for December 24th, 1898

Very passable rhubarb crumble at dinner, which is perplexing because we have no rhubarb preserved and no rhubarb has been in the shops these many months. I am tempted to enquire with cook but I do not wish to appear foolish. It is always possible that it was not rhubarb, but something identical to it in taste, appearance and texture. I may make a discreet inspection of the kitchen after the servants have retired. I shall explain away my absence from the bedroom by telling Simpkins that I have to make an extended tour of the house in order to exercise my thighs.

(I suppose as a philosophical speculation it could be argued that anything that is identical to rhubarb in taste, appearance and texture *is* rhubarb, but as a man of science I try to avoid the metaphysical because it is too abstract and gives me a sense of discomfort.)

My First Nocturnal Emission

BY

JEREMY SELMAN-TROYTT

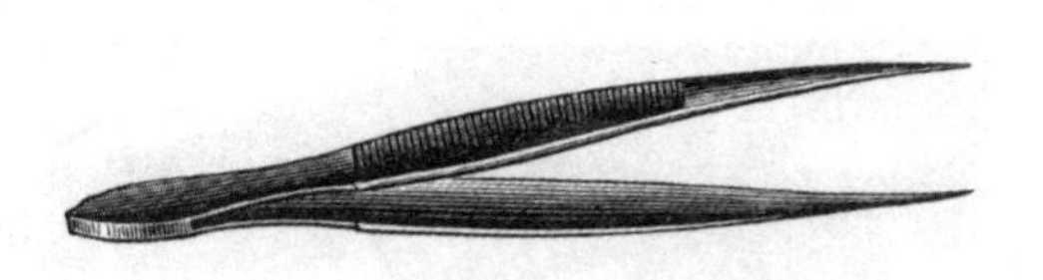

O'Rourke & LeFevre
London
MDCCCXCVIII

Foreword

I HAVE BEEN CRITICISED HEAVILY for not publishing this manuscript earlier, the accusation being that I have deprived a reading public of material that is both morally uplifting and medically informative. I deny the allegation entirely, and will endeavour to silence my critics by asking them whether they believe sincerely that I should have concentrated my energies upon this, my newest memoir, at the expense of completing the most recent volume of those memoirs that make up the collection known as 'The Soiling Series', variously titled *The First Time I Soiled My Trousers*, *The Second Time I Soiled My Trousers*, *The Third Time I Soiled My Trousers*, &c. ? For that is the simple choice that faced me: had I begun work on this account any sooner then the opening chapters of the first part of *The Fourteenth Time I Soiled My Trousers* would have lain neglected, unpublished, and unread upon my study shelves. While I had every moral motive and good intention for wishing to place in print as soon as possible those details of my first nocturnal emission, I could not in all conscience leave my last soiling undescribed, nor the series incomplete thus far. Any man, I am convinced, faced with a similar dilemma would have made the same choice. I now consider the matter closed and will enter into no more correspondence on the subject.

J. S-T

PART I

PREPARATIONS

CHAPTER ONE

I Go To Bed

In which the author describes his retiral to sleep

ALTHOUGH I AM SOMEWHAT LOATH to acknowledge my tardiness in this regard, it is an established fact that my first nocturnal emission did not occur until the night of November Twenty-First 1897, when I had already reached my twenty-ninth year. Whilst I accept this to be laggardly, even *unnatural* in a scientific sense (while being, of course, in its contemplation morally repellent absolutely!), I ascribe my lack of precocity in this experience to an enormous blow to the testicles which I received during a chess match in my thirteenth year. For some considerable time following this incident my testes were swollen and painful and it was as much as I was able to achieve merely to walk slowly with my thighs slightly apart. Certain other pursuits were denied me completely and it was to be nearly ten years before I was able to cross my legs whilst wearing trousers. Thus it was, having long considered my testicles to be redundant and inconvenient, that I should be completely unprepared for the events which occurred on that late autumnal evening some sixteen years later.

In accordance with household custom I was undressed by my valet, Simpkins, who then rubbed both my legs with a rough sponge in order to promote a healthy circulation of blood. With both legs invigorated I donned my cambric night-shirt and retired to bed betimes, for I had endured a taxing day of letter-writing to both of my Great Aunts.

Fairbanks, my butler, at my request fetched a cup of cocoa and a ship's biscuit, a culinary combination of my own devising calculated to soothe both stomach and brain into sufficient tranquillity to make easy that pleasant transition into sleep. I satisfied myself with both comestibles and cannot therefore connect to dyspepsia any of what happened subsequently.

The clock wanted three minutes of ten when I extinguished my candle. By eight minutes past I was asleep, a fact I can recount with both accuracy and authority because I insist that Fairbanks sit by my bed nightly in order to record the exact moment at which I fall asleep. (Parenthetically, I may add that it is my intention to publish a monograph upon the subject, having now accumulated data from over six thousand nights.)

If my night was dream-filled then I have no recollection of it, for nothing served to disrupt the tranquillity of my slumbers as far as I am able to recall. Nor was I unduly restless, for Simpkins, who is instructed to observe me sleeping and make notes in the appropriate journal, recorded:

> *Master turned no more than six times, and sighed but once, between nine minutes past ten (when Mr. Fairbanks had called me to my observation post) and half past eight the next morning*

when Master awoke. His breathing was easy, with no phlegm sounding in his airways nor mucus upon the pillow. There was no speech beyond a muffled refrain or two and none that could be made sense of. Master's night-cap remained in place . . .

In short, therefore, it was a night similar to those experienced by countless readers, where one has no conscious awareness of anything between closing one's eyes to sleep and then opening them again the following morning.

Frankly, my unruffled sleep came as some surprise because I had spent a goodly portion of the previous day concerned about an unpleasant swelling that had gathered beneath my left eye and which resembled nothing so much as a hen's egg, although not in the colour of it for it was a kind of mottled vermilion run through with veins of other colours and Dr. Twimsatt opined that it

(Eleven hundred and ninety-three pages here omitted. Ed.*)*

coming to consciousness slowly I was not at first aware of anything amiss. It was not until I turned my body slightly whilst stretching that I experienced a slight but strange sensation in my loins. Reaching down to explore the phenomenon I encountered a small area of resistance within the soft folds of my night-shirt. My first thought was that it might be a portion of ship's biscuit – perhaps dropped the night before and lodged in the cloth. However, one slight touch was enough to dispel this misconception. With a sense of complete repugnance I realised that the tip of my penis was adhering to the fabric of my night-shirt! I believe I must have screamed aloud because Simpkins was at my side in a trice. I bade him investigate my nether regions whilst I lay prone; notwithstanding the fear and disgust I felt at what may be encountered in his explorations, the need for scientific explanation took precedence as always.

Slowly lifting my night-shirt, he was able to detach it from my prepuce with a gentle tug (which caused me a shudder of complete revulsion) and then to examine the stiff and discoloured area of cloth with a magnifying glass. Then, gently rolling back my prepuce, he explored my glans. Throughout this ordeal I lay quiet, not wishing to disturb his careful analysis, although a thousand urgent questions pounded my fevered brain. Many of them centred on the pivotal question: what could have occurred? Of course at that time I made no connection between an involuntary ejaculation and my ruined testicles and so my thoughts ran to darker matters not at all to be associated with the mind of a man of science.

Finally, after more than twenty minutes of exploration – during which he twice measured the diameter of my testicles with callipers – Simpkins announced: 'I believe your gonads have emptied themselves, Master. But,' he added, 'I should like to call upon Mr. Fairbanks for a second opinion.' I was amazed, and nodded my consent in a state of distractedness. Could my testicles, in truth, have emptied themselves? And, if so, what might be the effect upon their proportions?

Fairbanks arrived with Mrs Fairbanks (to assist him in his examination by passing him those various implements he requested) and their eldest daughter Sarah to fetch and hold a bowl of water. Then Milly was summoned from the scullery to lay a fire to ward off the chill encroaching upon my lower section, which lay exposed to the cold air of the room and was without the benefit of covering.

Slowly and painstakingly Fairbanks repeated the analysis already undertaken by Simpkins, but in addition he applied a tourniquet to the top of my scrotum: an action which he preceded by an apology but which caused me to gasp in spite of the warning. Finally he looked up and nodded once to confirm Simpkins' findings: 'There can be no doubt, Sir', he said. 'Your testes have reduced in volume by three-eighths of a cubic inch on the left, and four-fifths on the right. Both Mrs Fairbanks and myself are astounded of course, although heartily pleased on your behalf.'

I confirm that this is a true account of the events of twenty-first and twenty-second of November 1887, and for those who express doubt I can provide proof in the form of the night-shirt itself (which I have had preserved under glass at the Royal Society) and several affidavits attesting to events having occurred just as I have recounted them, and variously signed by Simpkins (valet), Fairbanks and Mrs Fairbanks (butler and housekeeper respectively), their daughter Sarah (housemaid), Milly Lampeter (scullery maid), Jode Grafton (groom), and my distinguished neighbour Sir Walter Cornelius MP, DSO, KBE., all of whom were eventual witnesses to the removal of the night-shirt.

J. S-T 1898

J. SELMAN-TROYTT, ESQ.,
14 BERKELEY SQUARE, LONDON, W.

Dr. Sigmund Freud,
Berggasse 19,
Vienna A-1090,
Austria

22 December, 1898

Dear Sir,

I am in receipt of your letter of 4th *ult.* and found it confusing and annoying in equal measure. The reasons for my irritation were severalfold, and I shall enumerate them clearly and distinctly for you as follows:

First, your letter is in German. Yet I am English (as you must know, having written to me in England!). Therefore I speak English. To me this seems logical. I have no German, and I deem your presumption that I should both arrogant and insulting. This breach of good manners alone was sufficient grounds for discarding your letter unread but, rather than display an arrogant pomposity the equal of yours, I opted to find a way of reading what you had sent, thereby displaying the polite consideration that is as much a part of my nature as it is so manifestly lacking in your own.

This caused me no small amount of inconvenience, as there is an understandable paucity of people with your tongue among my colleagues. Therefore the matter of translation necessitated my speaking to several less familiar persons. This alone wasted valuable time. Eventually, a translation was obtained by my footman from a local tradesperson, a foreigner and native of Bremen who supplies us with tallow and matting at Michaelmas.

However, whilst I have little doubt that his German was equal to the task of reading your letter to himself, his English is exceedingly poor, and what I received from him in translation was so riven with ambiguities, lacunae and repetitions that I was required to read it above a dozen times in order to extrapolate some kind of sense. Even now I am unable to decipher your meaning in parts. This exercise wasted even more time, a commodity of which I am in very short supply, and which I prefer to invest in more valuable pursuits, such as scientific exploration. In any future correspondence, I would deem it a natural courtesy if you confined yourself to writing to me in English, a language with a vocabulary more than equal to the task of communicating even the most complex of scientific investigations. If you do not, then I shall discard your letters unread.

Second, you appear to be labouring under the misapprehension that I am Jewish. I am not. I have no idea from whence this misconception sprang. I am Anglo-Saxon. I have not a drop of Jewish blood in my veins and resent the implication that I do. This affront notwithstanding, your mistaken assumption that I am Jewish renders your letter wholly redundant, since your enquiries and concerns expressed therein refer to a situation of which I have absolutely no experience.

For example, when relating the details of your patient's nocturnal emission on the 11th August last, you ask me to advance an opinion on the emotional repercussions of his awakening to discover his glans adhering to a bed sheet (if such is an accurate translation of 'Er entdeckte dass seine Eichel an der Bettdecke klebte'). Yet how could I be expected to advise you with regard to a situation I have never experienced myself? A proper reading of my work – or at least a reading not blinded by preconceptions as to my ancestry and its effects upon my anatomy – will reveal that I have experiences only of awakening to find my *prepuce* adhering to various things . . . *not* my glans. Your letter assumes, *ipso facto*, that I am *sans* prepuce. I am not. Your considerate recognition of this fact at outset would have saved us both considerable time.

Third, I am bemused by your sudden reference to your patient's dreams of the preceding night. I am at an absolute loss as to the connection between the man's glans and his dream – *unless he was dreaming of his glans*! This reference is a mystifying *non sequitur*.

Even more galling is your pride and vanity in assuming that I am familiar with your work. I am not familiar with it. I have never even heard of *you*, much less your work. Unless your work falls within my specialisations of lotion research and auto-observation then it is highly unlikely that I will have read it. Even if the subject matter were interesting, it would require to be of the same standard as the work of Stanleyson and Montague before I would wish to absorb it. This is because I am possessed of *very* limited reading time, as I am extremely close to a breakthrough in my search for a prepuce retractor (as you will no doubt be aware if you have read *my* work!).

I have no experience of dreams beyond a single recurring illusion that my legs conform to a conventional shape. Possibly you have had the same dream? During this particular year, this dream has occurred on the nights of February 10th, June 8th, and August 22nd only. On all other nights I sleep soundly and with perfect ease. Accordingly, I cannot offer an opinion on anything you ask, even if I were disposed to look favourably upon your request that I do so.

Your parting comments on my work were welcome but I am afraid they were too generalised, and you made me labour too hard to receive them. In future I would strongly advise that you preface your requests for assistance and discussion with compliments that can be accessed with greater ease.

Yours &c.
J. Selman-Troytt

Romance

Mary Fortinbras

Mary launched an extraordinary period in Jeremy's life, for she was the subject of his first ever relationship with a woman. Their affair began in 1898 when Jeremy was already thirty. He was encouraged into forming this first amorous association by certain events referred to in his journals and texts*. He fixed upon Mary Fortinbras – the daughter of Charles Fortinbras, a Protestant sock manufacturer from Hartlepool.

But while Mr. Fortinbras approved of the liaison in principle, in actuality he proved to be the greatest obstacle to its consummation. For so protective was he of Mary, and so insistent that no accident should befall her, that he accompanied her everywhere, at every hour of the day, not even leaving her side to answer a call of nature.

So it was that Jeremy found himself not in the peaceful *liaison à deux* he had envisioned, but sucked into a stressful *ménage à trois*. Mr. Fortinbras, often much bored with the young couple's halting words of endearment and with Jeremy's explanations of his scientific investigations, would suddenly intervene and tax Jeremy for his opinion upon the latest political or economic affairs – opinions which Jeremy, as a man of science, felt unqualified to render – and the silences would sometimes stretch unbroken for six hours together.

---

* *My First Nocturnal Emission*, Jeremy Selman-Troytt, O'Rourke & LeFevre, London, 1898. See p.69.

J. SELMAN-TROYTT, ESQ.,
14 BERKELEY SQUARE, LONDON, W.

Rt. Hon. W. E. Gladstone,
Hawarden Castle,
Flintshire,
Wales

8 January, 1899

Dear Sir,

Please allow me to return the compliment by wishing a prosperous New Year to you, too, as well as to Mrs Gladstone (unless she be no longer alive).

I have perused your letter a score of times, and will endeavour to provide a simple explanation.

First, let me offer my reassurances that your footman is in no physical danger. None. You say the skin is 'sloughing off'. This is not unusual among older household staff. Many domestic servants shed whole layers of outer skin in short periods, replenishing the lost skin quickly from a hard, horny layer called 'keratin' located deep within the skin itself. The loss is hastened by many hours spent in moist, cool places like basements, shaded from direct sunlight. You may have experienced a similar effect yourself if you have kept your hand inserted somewhere moist for a lengthy time, or remarked a wrinkling of your fingertips when they are kept for long periods under a fresh poultice.

The condition can be messy, but it is not painful. You may reassure the man's family of that. Furthermore, there is no danger of the man's skin 'disappearing completely to expose his organs below', so the fears you express on that count are groundless. Just try to keep him warm and dry.* The sloughing should then stop of its own accord.

Please tender my condolences to him and his family. However, I believe he should consider himself most lucky that he has you for comfort and guidance when such incidents occur.

I remain your most humble and obedient servant,
J. Selman-Troytt

* As an interesting aside, there is some evidence that this advice may have been applied too enthusiastically, for when restoration work was carried out at Hawarden Castle in 1922 the mummified remains of a liveried servant were found inside the 'airing chamber' attached to the flue of the large kitchen range. Subsequent investigations by the coroner's office in nearby Holywell suggested these could have been Potts (the footman referred to in the above letter) since estate records for 1899 show that he was fined one shilling for allowing a part of his thumb to become detached and find its way into the Duke of Argyll's kedgeree while he was serving breakfast to guests. According to the ledger: 'Pots [*sic*] suspended for loosing [*sic*] more skin. Master furious. Sent him to kitchen to dry out all over.' The ledger contains no further mention of him so it seems safe to conclude, as the coroner did in 1922, that Potts was overcome by noxious fumes after placing himself in the 'airing chamber' and that his presence there went unnoticed by harried and overworked kitchen staff. As a consequence, it appears Potts 'dried out' beyond Gladstone's wildest expectations.

Family

Jonah and family c.1899

A rare *fin de siècle* photograph of the patriarchal Jonah at the head of his ever burgeoning family. His Austrian-born wife, Heilbron, was hand-picked by Josiah, both for her child-bearing girth and her resistance to pain. In order to prove the latter her domineering father, the Alpine industrialist von Kreemer, gave her twenty-five consecutive blows to the head with a heavy hammer in front of an openly admiring Jonah. When he saw that she was still conscious he seized her for his bride and had her transported to his marital bed to begin her child-bearing duties.

Note that the twenty-five year old James (back left) now sports a sprightly moustache, while his younger brother Jack proudly wears a new uniform with a jaunty 'pill-box'*. Between them stands their sister Jasmine, mother to ten-year-old Jesse (bottom left), who would go on to wear male clothing, change his name to 'Bill Fivestars', and pursue a career on the stage.** Jonah and Heilbron are flanked by Jill (left) and Jacqueline (right).

---

* Family records show that Jack had recently received his father's consent to begin work at Otis Elevators in Stockwell, London, finally allowing him to fulfill a lifelong ambition to become a lift attendant.

** Further information about Jeremy's descendants is available on the Selman-Troytt Appreciation Society website at: http://www.selman-troytt.com.

Family

John & Jonas Selman-Troytt

Together with Jonah, John (left) and Jonas (below) formed the infamous Triumvirate that was to spearhead the distribution of *Selman-Troytt Putty* to all parts of the British Empire in the last quarter of the 19th century.*

Their business tactics were an irresistible combination of imaginative flair and extreme ruthlessness. Jonas created a new slogan to appeal to the colonial purchaser ('*Fit for a Maharajah's windows*') while John systematically broke the legs of everyone who entered their offices. Within a very short time they grew to dominate the world's markets.

In Britain they enjoyed a total monopoly and many were the glaziers 'persuaded' into increasing their orders, often to three or four times their actual annual putty requirement, so that the unused surplus simply hardened in their bulging pockets.

* See Appendix VI on p.269 for more information about 19th century glazing.

Family

Jocelyn Selman-Troytt

Jocelyn, the eleventh son born to Lady Bethany, was a considerable disappointment to Josiah.

A very large baby (he weighed 28 lbs* at birth), he had required forceps in a delivery so challenging that the doctor in charge of the confinement was exhausted at its conclusion.

As Jocelyn grew, his body slowly developed enough strength to hold his head upright, but his eyes never moved in unison and he displayed much less mental acuity than his brothers. For example, he never spoke, infuriating his father and sparking speculation that the pressure of the birth forceps may have damaged his capability for language. This was a distinct possibility, for the deep marks from the forceps were visible in his skull right into adulthood. As a schoolboy he often had difficulty removing his cap because its band had become lodged in the grooves.

Although no medical records exist, Josiah's oft-repeated comment that '*The boy's seed cannot be allowed to spread*', together with an entry in Jeremy's own journal – '*Sterilised Jocelyn today.*' – suggest that Jocelyn may well have been the recipient of a procedure to prevent him from fathering children.

---

* 12.7kg

Family

Jarvis Selman-Troytt – 1864–?

Jeremy's brother Jarvis was misplaced in the summer of 1868, during an excursion to view the primate enclosure in Regent's Park Zoo. When the large group of Selman-Troytt children returned home, accompanied by a harried governess, it was discovered that Jarvis was no longer with them. The police were called but a thorough search of the zoo revealed no trace of him.

Over the next twenty years there were numerous claimants purporting to be the missing Jarvis, hoping thereby to gain a share of the Selman-Troytt fortune. The most credible candidate was Gordon McDiarmid (right, seated) whose 'father' claimed to have found him wandering alone in the primate enclosure of Regent's Park Zoo in July 1868.

Jeremy's forensic skills were called upon and he made a meticulous set of measurements during a microscopic full-body examination. Although the examination took nine hours, he pronounced the results '*inconclusive*', despite the sickle-shaped birthmark behind Gordon's right ear, a birth defect shared by seven other Selman-Troytt children.

Accordingly, the family decided to reject his claim, reasoning that it was better to be safe than sorry where family assets were concerned.

Journal notes for May 23rd, 1900

Miss Fanshawe and her mother to tea on Sunday next!

Journal notes for May 28th, 1900

Tea strained! Father emitted an audible faux pas which made Miss Fanshawe blush and flap her fan vigorously. Father roared with delight at her discomfiture and then asked if any of her relations were Bantus. It was an awkward moment and I almost spoke. However the opportunity passed before I could marshal my thoughts and so I gave her an extra scone by way of apology. She left shortly thereafter, although she seemed quite stiff with Father and when he tried to take her hand she gave him the one with the scone in it.

Journal notes for July 1st, 1900

Hennessy has called again re. ectoplasm. He says his mouth is filled with it and that a quantity is escaping. He sought my assurance that I could see it emerging, but I could not.

What *is* ectoplasm? Have I any in *my* mouth?

Journal notes for July 27th, 1900

Miss O'Shaughnessy to tea next Sunday. I made the invitation by note, passed to her by a companion while she was at prayer. She accepted with a simple nod of her head, not wishing to interrupt her recitations. High hopes! I shall ask cook to bake a special cake so that our mouths may be moist enough to speak.

Romance

Kathleen O'Shaughnessy

Selman-Troytt's relationship with Miss Kathleen O'Shaughnessy (left) was difficult from its inception in 1900, in part because of her intense God-fearing piety that would not suffer Jeremy to approach within '*an offensive distance*', but mainly because of Josiah's outspoken disapproval. His staunch Presbyterian beliefs, fixed immovably by the short sermon he had heard on the only occasion he went to church, were offended by her family's '*elaborate and tawdry*' Catholicism.

In consequence, Selman-Troytt's first invitation for her to take tea with his parents was an occasion where all parties found it difficult to relax. There was a palpable sectarian tension in the room. It was Josiah who broke first under its influence, just as Miss O'Shaughnessy was removing her coat. '*I'll have no Fenian scum in this house*,' he screamed to all assembled, '*and no son of mine will consort with that rabid whore of Satan.*' So saying, he snatched her prayer book and threw it on the fire with a roar of victory. He then had her forcibly ejected from the house by four footmen who hurled her into the street.

Afterwards, Jeremy endeavoured to make amends with a present accompanied by a tender letter: *My Dear Miss O'Shaughnessy. Please find enclosed a replacement prayer book. Also, a slice of the cake that you missed. I fear I must apologise for my father's brutality. Also for the dryness of the cake. Cook left it in the oven a little too long because she was distracted by news that her father had died. Sorry. I hope I may see you again. Affectionately Yours, Jeremy*. But her parents returned his package with a stiff note.

JOURNAL NOTES FOR AUGUST 24TH, 1900

Increasingly concerned about both knees. Have they been this big before?

JOURNAL NOTES FOR AUGUST 29TH, 1900

A curious day. This morning I awoke with the urgent desire to invent a cure for baldness, even though I am not bald. I mixed a preparation in what seemed like little time and it was so potent that rubbing some on the backs of my hands produced a luxuriant pelt within fifteen minutes. The only drawback was that the hair grew dense, short and soft, not unlike a short-haired cat. Also, the colour was a flaming red. Then I awoke to discover my previous awakening had taken place in a dream, as though I were awakening from an inner dream of which I had no knowledge! I find myself frightened at the prospect of being excluded from myself in this way, for who knows what happened within the inner chamber? Slight trembling. Feelings of nervousness.

JOURNAL NOTES FOR OCTOBER 20TH, 1900

Recommenced experimentation with belladonna and various other extracts. Once again a sensation of nasal widening. When I looked at my reflection I could see no eyes in my face, which was unsettling.

JOURNAL NOTES FOR OCTOBER 22ND, 1900

When I walked into the hallway today I was certain I saw a cat; yet when I looked again there was nothing there! A mystery.

Journal notes for October 23rd, 1900

Saw the cat again, but, as before, when I blinked it was no longer there.

Do we own a cat? I must ask Fairbanks.

Journal notes for October 24th, 1900

Cat again.

Journal notes for October 25th, 1900

And again.

Journal notes for October 26th, 1900

No cat!

Journal notes for October 27th, 1900

No cat again. I am thankful it has gone. I have never been fond of cats since Cholpley was attacked by one which lacerated his lobes. I wonder whose it was.

I have today read of the French condition *ennui* and discovered that I have had it!

Patients

Cecil Albert Cavanaugh, Lord Dunstan

Lord Dunstan first consulted Selman-Troytt in 1898 concerning his congenital lack of chin. The Dunstan chin had been receding for generations, but by the time it reached Cecil Cavanaugh it had disappeared altogether. It took an enormous effort of concentration for him to bring his lips together, making speech difficult and the retention of saliva a challenge for the want of a watertight seal around his mouth.

Selman-Troytt accepted the challenge and fashioned a prosthetic chin from African ivory. The prosthesis incorporated a hollowed centre that functioned as a 'chin cup' and which collected any 'overflow saliva' that Lord Dunstan was unable to retain. When full, the 'chin cup' could be emptied discreetly by way of a small spigot located on the underside. During soirees or parliamentary debates Lord Dunstan would often absent himself in order to empty his chin before it overflowed and stained his suit.

Apart from being stark white, hard and very shiny – not unlike a very large billiard ball – the prosthesis bore a remarkable resemblance to a natural chin and Dunstan was convinced that it was completely undetectable when attached by clamps to his side whiskers. It impeded his lip movement somewhat, and made his speech less intelligible than it had been previously, but Lord Dunstan was happy with the compromise. When people pointed out that his arguments had become difficult to follow he would try very hard to say: 'I should far rather be known as a man with a strong chin and weak opinion, than the other way around!'

The 'Dunstan chin prosthesis' was the first in a long line of parts which Selman-Troytt designed for bodily reconstruction. Ivory was his favourite material, and the scope of his prostheses grew along with his confidence until they encompassed whole limbs carved directly from a single tusk. He loved the sense of freedom and power that limb replacement gave him to improve upon Nature '*in the event that she show herself deficient.*' For example, in 1902 he made a matching pair of replacement legs for a sailor who had lost his own in a naval engagement. True to his philosophy, Selman-Troytt had them carved much longer than the originals, such that the man's height increased from 5' 4" to 8' 6"*. As an act of Christian charity, Selman-Troytt then had his own tailor fashion new trousers for the man in order to assist him with the transition and to conceal the exceptionally long, gently curving prostheses from the gaze of curious onlookers.

* 162.5cm and 259cm respectively.

Patients

Mr. Butterfield

The enigmatic Mr. Butterfield (left), subject of three of Selman-Troytt's written works* and the man who submitted himself for examination on dozens of occasions as a direct challenge to Selman-Troytt to discover what was wrong with him. Butterfield never spoke or moved during examinations, so as to make diagnosis '*a fairer and more interesting test*'.

Selman-Troytt's initial diagnosis was alopecia, but Butterfield failed to react encouragingly when this was suggested (although he *did* suffer from alopecia, this was not the condition he was hoping to have diagnosed). In his later biography he described the initial alopecia diagnosis as '*hopelessly wide of the mark*', but suggested that Selman-Troytt was getting 'much warmer' with his later suggestion of blepharitis.**

Jeremy discontinued the consultations after Butterfield's 56th visit, despite the latter's exhotations that he should continue his investigations. Butterfield later wrote: '*I am not sure that he realised how close he came. On several occasions he was only inches away from the right spot. I tried hard to convince him to carry on because he was bound to make the correct diagnosis sooner or later, if only according to the law of averages.*'

---

* *Examining Mr. Butterfield* (3 vols), O'Rourke & LeFevre, London.

** Inflammation of the eyelids, characterized by flaky debris at the eyelash bases.

Patients

Charles Leonard Hennessy

The Hennessy parents, although wealthy, decided to continue to believe in God. As very strict Methodists they were opposed to any foods that were not mentioned explicitly in the Old Testament, so Hennessy père was often absent from home for long periods, shopping for groceries in the Levant.

Left alone with his mother, a stern woman who prayed constantly that her husband would return safely with a sufficient supply of dates, the very young Charles became increasingly convinced that a bubble of ectoplasm was emerging from his mouth, although no other family members could ever see it.

As an adult he would frequently call on acquaintances to ask if they could see the ectoplasm. When they answered in the negative he would leave crestfallen, but would usually return invigorated within a week or so to ask again.

In his autobiography (*Living with a Mouthful of Ectoplasm*, O'Rourke & LeFevre, 1914) he described the sensation as '*akin to having one's mouth filled with an ostrich egg . . . but without the shell, the weight or the yolk*'.

Selman-Troytt suddenly began to see the ectoplasm in 1901, which delighted Hennessy and gave him great reassurance. Thereafter he expressed his gratitude by becoming a patron and funding much of Selman-Troytt's remaining research work.

Contemporaries

Senhor Rodolpho & Senhora Juanita Brazin

Selman-Troytt treated Senhor Brazin (left) for Siebart's Disease, a condition which gave him chronic lip pain and forced him to speak in a whisper. He attempted to compensate by speaking through an amplification trumpet, but often became depressed by the difficulty of using it (it was over 6 feet (1.82m) in length and weighed 40lb (18kg). After a few minutes of speech his arms would become exhausted and he would need to lapse into silence, causing him immense frustration when he was in the middle of reciting Tennyson's *Morte D'Arthur*.

Over time his depression deepened, due to the large medical bills he received, and he began to suffer suicidal impulses that prompted him to sleep with a loaded pistol strapped to his head. His wife Juanita (right) did her best to dissuade him from taking his own life by reminding him that there was no money left with which to bury him properly – which would mean his anonymous burial in an unmarked pauper's grave.

When Rodolpho died suddenly whilst turning over in his sleep, Juanita refused to allow the event to dent her natural *joie de vivre*. Freed of the need to apply salve to his lips every five minutes, she threw herself back into a hectic social life. She finally died as she had lived, entertaining a small crowd with an anecdote about Rodolpho's misplaced spare trousers.

J. SELMAN-TROYTT, ESQ.,
14 BERKELEY SQUARE, LONDON, W.

Sir Cuthbert Wheen,
The Redoubt,
Higham,
nr. Rochester,
Kent

7 August, 1901

Dear Sir,

I thank you for the information on your preputial adhesions. I can free these for you at a modest cost of one guinea per adhesion, or a total of eleven guineas.

An alternative home remedy, as you say you are incapacitated and unable to travel, would be for you to do this for yourself by pushing the handle of a teaspoon down between glans and prepuce and working it gently from side to side until the adhesions are freed. For preference the spoon handle should be *smooth* and *rounded*, rather than bearing sharp edges or an angular family crest.

If you wish me to carry out the procedure professionally using *my* spoon, then I will insist that you sanitise your glans before your arrival here.

My compliments to Mrs Wheen.

Your humble and obedient servant,
J. Selman-Troytt

J. Selman-Troytt, Esq.,
14 Berkeley Square, London, W.

Professor Miles Stanleyson,
Kotherschaft Institute,
Rellerphelz Str.,
Geneva,
Switzerland

27 October, 1901

Dear Sir,

You may be aware that I have written to you in the past. I have accompanied each letter with samples of my own skin cells, taken scrupulously under laboratory conditions. According to my calculations, the combined weight of these samples has reached a total of 3 lb 7 oz* since 1890. However, I cannot seem to trace a reply from you.

I appreciate that you are very busy, but would be most grateful if you could find time to examine my correspondence in order to provide an answer to the question I posed in my letter dated 19 February, 1890.**

Thanking you for your indulgence I remain,

Your most obedient servant,
J. Selman-Troytt

* 1.55 kilograms

** See p.16

Romance

Thomas Cartwright & Lesley Carrington

One of the greatest scandals to break over the Selman-Troytt family was the revelation that the demure Miss Lesley Carrington (below), Jeremy's fiancée from 1902 to 1903, was none other than his long-standing acquaintance, the amateur chemist and raconteur Thomas Cartwright (left). Fortunately this fact did not emerge until some twenty years after Jeremy's death.

Astounding as it may appear, it is now clear that Jeremy had absolutely no knowledge that his friend and his fiancée were the same person. Even more astounding is that there were occasions when he would leave Thomas drinking in their club in order to escort Miss Carrington for the evening, before then returning to his club for a 'nightcap' with Thomas. Exactly how Mr. Cartwright managed these evenings remains a mystery.

Romance

Sylvia Lamont-Hughes

Sylvia (left), holding the doves which Jeremy presented to her as a symbol of his devotion upon the occasion of their first speaking at a Savoy Hotel *thé dansant*.* Sylvia was said to be '*touched by the gesture*' but '*appalled by the staining*'.

The doves soon refused to be parted from her. She and Jeremy would take an afternoon stroll through Hyde Park, chatting about his latest researches, whilst a dove perched contentedly on each of her outstretched arms.

Throughout their extensive peregrinations other birds, encouraged by the sight, would be tempted to alight upon her as well, until she resembled '*nothing so much as a ledge at St. Pancras Station*', as Jeremy later described the scene to his friend Guscott. On one occasion, he recounted, she carried forty birds on each arm, such that '*her arms finally gave way and their squawking drowned me out. The soiling was astounding.*'

* See pp.192-3 in *Social & Sexual Etiquette* for Selman-Troytt's views on the merits of avian and other gifts.

Romance

Lucinda Purefoy-McKinlay

Encouraged by Sylvia's response to the doves, Jeremy impulsively presented Miss Purefoy-McKinlay (left) with a large African Grey parrot as a means of beginning a conversation when they encountered each other strolling outside the Crystal Palace at Penge.

Lucinda was enchanted, and within hours she had thrust Harrods into a state of momentary *non-plus* by demanding cuttlefish '*by the yard, and as fast as you can dry it.*'

The bird's history caused her some inconvenience, however, for it had once been owned by a retired naval captain, late of the Tasman Sea. In consequence, it would punctuate gloomy silences by screaming out the word '*Scrotum!*' repeatedly, a practice which caused passing pedestrians to blench when Lucinda promenaded along Bond Street with the parrot perched regally upon her right shoulder. When her flow of social invitations began to subside as a result, Lucinda had the bird destroyed without hesitation.

Jeremy, now thirty-six, was despondent. '*I shall give no more birds as love tokens*,' he confided to a breathless and wheezing Lenoir*, '*for upon balance they have brought me nothing but pain and disgrace. The distraction of both has affected my search for a scientific breakthrough.*'

---

* See p.28

J. SELMAN-TROYTT, ESQ.,
14 BERKELEY SQUARE, LONDON, W.

Hon. Percy Trowbridge,
Heston Chambers,
Great Ormond St.,
London, W.

2 July, 1903

Trowbridge,

I am in receipt of another of your letters containing 'news' of you, your family and your acquaintances. This makes three such letters you have sent me this month alone, and over seventeen since the year began.

As you are aware, I have asked you repeatedly to refrain from sending me such letters. My writing time in any day is limited, my time for correspondence even more so, which is why I endeavour to confine my correspondence to the non-trivial in the time I have available.

Trusting I will hear no more from you I remain,

Your affectionate friend,
J. Selman-Troytt

J. SELMAN-TROYTT, ESQ.,
14 BERKELEY SQUARE, LONDON, W.

Sir Adrian Mumble,
Mumble Hall,
Sussex

23 August, 1904

Sir,

I am in receipt of your letter and, to speak frankly and earnestly, I must express my intense irritation that you should now seek clarification of instructions discussed already at great length in my rooms; instructions which I had my assistant repeat dozens of times to your wife, requesting confirmation from her that she had understood each sentence before the next was commenced.

I make no apology for being short with you, for I am extremely busy with my researches and find myself on the point of a breakthrough. To be asked to repeat myself now, and without remuneration, on a series of matters which you too confirmed were clear in your understanding, is irksome in the extreme.

Now, with that point made, let me reiterate certain of the instructions made to you already. The following references to the points raised in your letter will clarify your misconceptions.

1. Your parts 1, 5 & 7 are correct, with the proviso that you have substituted 'serge' for 'surge'. This will not do. Such confusion or substitution could have unexpected consequences.
2. Your part 19 is correct in its entirety.
3. Your part 3 is wrong from outset to conclusion. Strike it fully.

You will need to hold both parts clear of the ground while your wife holds the end; not the other way around! Common sense should dictate this anyway – how would you propose to hold your *wife* clear of the ground?

4. Your part 3a. In this clause (surely it would have been less confusing to label it 'part 4'!) you have mistakenly substituted 'feet' for 'inches'. Such as you describe would be wholly impossible given those dimensions.
5. Your part 4. Your wife will need to use the tips of forefinger and thumb as a type of loose clamp. As her left hand will be occupied (this highlights another misconception of yours, since your part 14 refers to her right hand when it should refer to her left) this must perforce involve the utilisation of her right hand. Should she lack sufficient dexterity in her right hand, then it is permissible to delegate this task to a servant.
6. Your part 14. 'right' should read 'left'. See above.
7. Your part 5. You have misunderstood the intention. Both of your own feet need to be spaced slightly apart, to sustain balance and help to spread the load should it become necessary.
8. Your part 6. You can make the second fold by moving towards one another. There is no need for the intervention of a third party, as you suggest. A mnemonic may assist you both. ('**C**alico **C**urtains **W**ith **I**nde**F**inable **S**callops **S**tretc**H**ing **F**ro**M** **L**and's **E**nd to **K**rakatoa' would give you the correct order, although you may chose to compose your own.)
9. Your part 8. The order is as discussed with me in my rooms. Not left, left, forward, left, left, left as you assert (since I suspect that would position you in an adjacent room) but left, *right*, forward, left, left, left. Again, this is a matter of simple common sense.
10. Your part 9. Again you have misunderstood the intention. Any moisture can be dabbed away with gauze.
11. Your part 10. Slight seepage is to be expected at this juncture, although your wife may need this explained to her again and again before she becomes convinced. If she becomes agitated or

exhibits fear then stroking her forehead and crooning may calm her. In other respects this part is correct.

12. Your part 11. Strike this entirely. It has no place here, and was certainly never referred to by me. Is it possible that in your confusion you are conflating two conversations held with different people at different times? I am speculating. Have you engaged in another conversation recently, perhaps on a nautical theme? 'Sheets' in this context could be read as a reference to 'ropes', such as those used on board ship. Beyond this, I am at a loss. My own reference to 'sheets' in your part 6 was correct, but that was my only reference to 'sheets'.
13. Your part 12. Once again, it is your own knees that should be slightly bent, no one else's! We covered this exhaustively. If this position is uncomfortable for you when maintained for longer than an hour, then some kind of strapping is permissible. Once again, your wife's knees do not come into this. Please strike them.
14. Your parts 13–15. Strike entirely. Again this seems to be a conflation of separate conversations (or a gross misunderstanding). At no time during our conversation did I make reference to anyone other than you or your wife – with the possible exception of a servant. Your wife will need to be made to see this. Remember: if she has difficulty comprehending or retaining the information, then your main ally is repetition.
15. Your part 16. Your wife will have to overcome her feminine sensibilities for the greater good. That is the simple beginning and end of the matter. This is not a situation where any party is gifted the luxury of choice, but one in which necessity holds sway.

I trust the foregoing will have clarified your confusion once and for all. Any further explanations you demand will need to be charged for at my usual rate.

Your most humble and obedient servant,

J. Selman-Troytt

J. SELMAN-TROYTT, ESQ.,
14 BERKELEY SQUARE, LONDON, W.

Miss Emmelina Clacker-Satterby,
43, Strand,
London, W.

26 May, 1904

My Dearest Miss Clacker-Satterby,

I thank you for your reply of the 24th *inst.*

It was both touching and welcome. Your words of endearment make me hopeful that I may not be incorrect in interpreting such sentiments as signs of encouragement that I may proceed with my suit.

I too look forward to being able to converse with you at some point in the future, which I hope will not be too distant! I am involved in very exciting research work on a lightweight prepuce retractor and should welcome the opportunity to regale you with the points of greatest interest from the past twenty years. The work is complicated but I would do my utmost to simplify it so that it would remain within the bounds of your comprehension.

I am advised by colleagues that a conversation with a woman can never prove as interesting as that with a man because of the gulf in intellect and interests; however I hope you will not regard me as too forward if I should proffer the compliment that in your case I should welcome the opportunity to prove the assertion false!

I, too, long to see you again. Like you, I am excited at the prospect. Like you I count the days. Also like you, I think of you often. Your kind words about my legs I regard as indicative of the depth of your sensibilities and they serve to confirm me in my initial assessment that you will prove to be a model wife: soft-hearted, warm, kind, and chaste. I hope sincerely that we may find a connection on an intellectual plane, as well as on a physical one, and my happiness will be doubled if you find my retractor as exciting and stimulating as I do.

Your invitation for me to take tea with you and your mother is one I should be delighted to accept if it will smooth the path towards our eventual union. As I explained in my initial letter, procreation is my primary intention with regard to my search for a wife. However, I had understood your letter to say that your mother was deceased, so either I have misunderstood your letter or misunderstood the nature of the assembly. Please advise, by return, whether it is a social gathering or an opportunity for mourning, so that I may dress accordingly. Thank you.

I shall call upon you at half past four, as suggested in your letter.*

Yours, with intense and burning affection,
Jeremy Selman-Troytt

* According to contemporary accounts the meeting did take place, but the relationship foundered when Emmelina failed to reciprocate Selman-Troytt's enthusiasm for the prepuce retractor.

Journal notes for June 30th, 1905

Yet another success! Softened two seed pods with only one application, this time upon the ridges. Very encouraged.

Cook came to me with fourth request to change regular brand of meat paste. I refused again. She seems determined, but she will not win. I am determined to be steadfast and she underestimates my obstinacy.

More news of erectile dysfunction floods in with each passing day*. I am not without sympathy. Can I help, beyond counselling? My research is at maximum capacity already.

Checked post today. Still no reply from Stanleyson. I sent Fairbanks to enquire at the post office.

Journal notes for August 9th, 1905

Father is very old already. According to current actuarial statistics published in *The Times* this morning, he should be dead. I considered speaking to him about it this afternoon, but upon deliberation I held my tongue.

There seems to be a lot of dust in the house. I have asked Rokeby to call and confirm this for me.

---

* Selman-Troytt published *Erectile Dysfunction – 1,684 Recorded Observations of Detumescence* in late 1904. It was well-received, both critically and in terms of sales, and caused another increase in the flow of clients to his practice and an expansion in his counselling repertoire.

JOURNAL NOTES FOR DECEMBER 12TH, 1905

Whilst giving Simpkins his weekly examination for balanitis I discovered that he had very severe rickets. I am very surprised that I had not noticed it before because when I looked closely at his legs I saw that when his ankles are together his knees are almost fifteen inches* apart, and the space between his legs is a perfect oval. I suspect this accounts for his unusual way of walking, a peculiar type of rolling gait that has occasionally reminded me of a chimpanzee holding a tea tray aloft in one hand. But again this was on the *periphery* of my thoughts and was not something that registered itself firmly in my consciousness. I suppose I have *seen* it, but not *noticed* it . . . an interesting distinction!**

I am considering whether it may be possible to bend his legs back straight with metal braces. Or is he too old? He thinks he is thirty-one, but does not know for certain. We know that he has been in the house for twenty-two years but has he no recollection of anything before that. I should be interested to assess if I could cure his condition, but I would not wish his legs to snap in the process.

---

* 37cm

** See the journal entry for August 29th, 1900 on p.90 for another of Selman-Troytt's tantalising forays into the philosophy of mind.

MISS LALLIA PATTERSON,
63 MARCHMONT TERRACE, LONDON, W.

Box 3872,
The Times Newspaper,
New Printing House Square,
Gray's Inn Road,
London, W.C.

14 January, 1906

Dear Sir,

I read your advertisement* in *The Times* and should like to respond by advising you that I fit the description and requirements specified. You sound both intriguing and attractive and I should be most interested to make your acquaintance.

In the hope of receiving your positive responses, I remain,

Yours faithfully,
Lallia Patterson (Miss)

* This is the first known occasion upon which Selman-Troytt used advertising in the 'personal' columns of newspapers to further his search for a spouse. See Appendix VII on p.271.

J. SELMAN-TROYTT, ESQ.,
14 BERKELEY SQUARE, LONDON, W.

Miss Lallia Patterson,
63 Marchmont Terrace,
London, W.

18 January, 1906

Dear Miss Patterson,

I was overjoyed to receive your forwarded response to my request for respondents to reply to the advertisement detailing my requirements with regard to applicants for the role of prospective spouse. I am very excited at the prospect that you may possess the physical and mental attributes specified.

I too should be most interested to learn more about you, whilst you, I am sure, would wish to know various details about me before any engagement can be announced officially.

My background is easily summarised. I am a man of independent means and good education, interested in all aspects of scientific research and observation but particularly in lotions and the workings and processes of the human body. I have few interests beyond these horizons, for my work is also my passion.

I speak only when necessary.

If we are to be joined in matrimony then it will be necessary for us to ensure that two compatibilities exist: namely, one between you and me, and another between you and my family, who will wish to ensure your suitability to enter our family and continue its good offices.

To those ends, may I extend an invitation for you to take tea with us on the Sunday after next at the above address, in order that our intercourse may be observed and commented upon by other family members? This will allow them to formulate opinions which they can contribute at our next family conference. The occasion will also afford the pair of us an excellent opportunity to discover the extent of our own compatibilities, which I hope, if I may so opine gallantly and in a complimentary fashion designed to flatter you without expressing any undue familiarity that you will find offensive, will be extensive.

May we say Sunday 28th at 4 o'clock in the afternoon?

I look forward with great anticipation and eagerness to meeting you, and my heart burns already at the prospect that our union may be blessed with attraction on both sides so that we may proceed to the necessary physical elements without repugnance.

With deepest affection,
Jeremy Selman-Troytt

MISS LALLIA PATTERSON,
63 MARCHMONT TERRACE, LONDON, W.

J. Selman-Troytt, Esq.,
14 Berkeley Square,
London, W.

20 January, 1906

Dearest Jeremy,

I find that my heart burns too! I hope you will not consider it forward or unseemly in a lady if I reveal to you that the passion in your letter made my heart beat faster. As I read each word my body began to tremble like a leaf and my brow became quite moist. These are sensations wholly unknown to me hitherto, for I own readily that I am still very young and without romantic experience.

I shall most happily accede to your request that I present myself at your home at 4 o'clock a week from tomorrow for tea with your family. I know that I shall count the minutes until that moment . . . and still discover they pass too slowly!

Yours with deepest affection . . . and perhaps even more,
Lallia

Journal notes for 22nd January, 1906

Miss Lallia Patterson has accepted my invitation to tea next Sunday! My advertisement specified my exact requirements, so I am very hopeful that she will possess the correct shape and disposition. Also, that her parts be right. I am convinced now that advertising supplies the most efficient means of finding an appropriate wife.

Since the arrival of her last letter I have been considering the situation in its entirety and, provided that we find ourselves mentally and physically compatible during tea, I cannot see why the matter should not be brought promptly to its logical conclusion by discussing the arrangements for our union. Therefore, I cannot see why, *mutatis mutandis*, our meeting at tea should not be regarded also as an occasion appropriate for a proposal to marry. Given that she meets my express requirements, I cannot see what purpose would be served by delay!

Therefore with Father's approval I shall propose to her at the conclusion of the meal. I shall speak with him about this when he appears calmer.

Very excited! It is difficult to comprehend that I may soon be joined with another! I yearn to begin noting down the sensations of such an experience.

Journal notes for 23rd January, 1906

Audience today with Father at which I acquainted him with the feelings that exist between Miss Patterson and me. I explained my plan to propose to her provided she meets with my approval, and asked for his consent to the match. He has given it, pending his own assessment over tea next Sunday!

He will examine her during the meal and then revert to me once he has concluded further discussions with John, Jonas and Jonah. Pending their decision I am to detain Miss Patterson in the library at the meal's conclusion, and we will then be able to proceed as they dictate. If I receive their consent then I shall propose to her immediately!

I do so hope they discover within her the same loving and gentle qualities which have impelled me towards her with increasing velocity.

Find myself feeling somewhat nervous about matters now, particularly about what will happen if my family's assessment runs counter to my own and they insist that she be rejected. In that event I am sure I shall be unsettled, particularly when it is already clear that we are compatible.

J. SELMAN-TROYTT, ESQ.,
14 BERKELEY SQUARE, LONDON, W.

Miss Lallia Patterson,
63 Marchmont Terrace,
London, W.

24 January, 1906

My Dearest Lallia,

I am in receipt of your letter dated 20th *inst.* and write to inform you that I have noted our appointment in my diary so that there is no possibility that I shall overlook it. I have instructed our cook to bake a special pound cake to mark the occasion of our first meeting. I hope that our feelings during the interview will enjoy sufficient florescence to render possible the revelation of a surprise I have been pondering, and which will be appropriate provided you are all that I hope you to be. I cannot speak more of this until after I have seen you in person, so would ask that you remain patient and do not press me upon this matter.

Until then I remain yours with deepest affection . . . and also something more, for I find that I yearn strongly for my first glimpse of your angelic countenance. Emotions, strangers hitherto in the life of a disinterested scientist, rise within me at the prospect of beholding your beauty.

Yours forever,
Jeremy

My First Involuntary Ejaculation

BY

JEREMY SELMAN-TROYTT

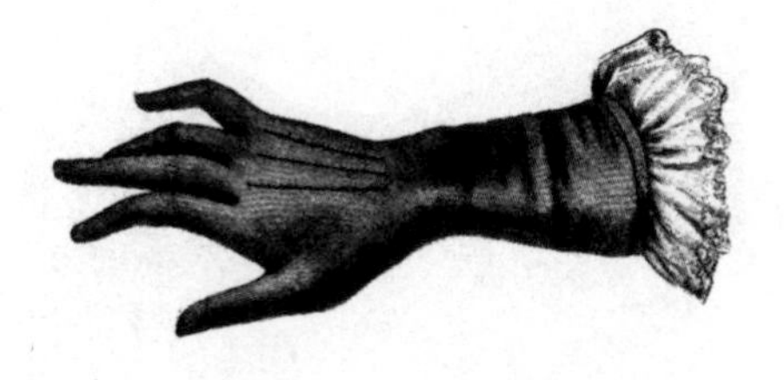

O'Rourke & LeFevre
London
MCMVII

Introduction

MY FIRST INVOLUNTARY EJACULATION I regard as wholly distinct from my first nocturnal emission*, the latter having taken place whilst I was unconscious and in no position to observe and record the relevant details that made my first conscious ejaculation so exciting from a scientific perspective.

In this volume I shall attempt a narrative account rather than a thesis, an account within which I shall relate events precisely as they unfolded without venturing too far into editorial conjecture concerning cause and effect with regard to why the ejaculation may have occurred. I do have my own theories on this point but would prefer to keep them *sub rosa* until they have been tested more thoroughly. Accordingly, I am certain that a second, shorter work** (devoid of anecdotal distractions and concentrating only on those facts germane to the outcome) will be necessary in order to synthesise the relevant elements into a cohesive proof comprehensive enough to be unassailable when subjected to rigorous scrutiny and moderation. The second volume I shall deal with according to the constraints of my normal routine and schedule. Until then, therefore, I must request the reader to content himself with following a chain of causality that I will own is both hypothetical and flimsier than I would wish. In essence, I shall ask him to accept as fact certain of my postulations with regard to why I may have ejaculated involuntarily.

I make no apology for this, for until I have the opportunity to

---

* See published excerpt from *My First Nocturnal Emission* on p.69.

** Published later as *My First Involuntary Ejaculation – Volume II.*

test each link in the causal chain to prove its authenticity and exactitude I am bound to fall back upon assumption. Furthermore, I must accept that doubt must, *ipso facto,* surround certain of those assumptions until they are proven to be correct.

Now, with that matter disposed of, let me proceed to the events in question.

PART I

A SIGN OF THINGS TO COME

CHAPTER ONE

I Wake Up

(In which the author comes to consciousness at the beginning of the day in question)

ALTHOUGH AUGURIES HAVE NO PART to play in the life of any scientist, had I chosen to make a prognostication about the significance of the day in question then there was ample material with which to prompt me.

I was roused at the customary time of 7:52 a.m., and allowed my coverlet to be smoothed by Fairbanks after he had turned me upon my back and sat me upright supported by fresh pillows. I was then presented with breakfast by Simpkins, my valet, who in laying the tray upon the counterpane was sufficiently maladroit to allow some tea to spill from the cup. In former times I would have upbraided him immediately for carelessness, but on this occasion I declined to mention it because I had recently decided upon a greater tolerance with regard to his undulating upper body movements.*

However, when I looked up in order to vouchsafe to him a small sign of forgiveness, I became aware that something was amiss with his left eye, for it was swollen, reddened and weeping, with partially closed lids that were discoloured, bruised and covered with excessive crustiness. His strenuous tensing of the cheek muscles below the eye suggested that it gave him great pain, while his efforts to lean his head back and to the right so that none of his ocular effusions dripped onto the breakfast tray were further evidence that he too was aware that there was something wrong with it.

It looked for all the world as though the injury had been inflicted by a punch or blow from an opponent, but I considered this unlikely as Simpkins remains in my room all night to record my sleeping behaviour. A fight taking place beside my bed would surely have awakened me.

When I asked him about its provenance he stated with conviction that he had noticed the condition himself only moments before and was mystified by it. He said that he could not account for it, other than to conclude that it had simply appeared of its own accord during the night. However, even as he said this I noted that an evasive quality had entered his manner and that his uninjured eye began to slide inwards in a guilty manner that suggested his account was at variance with the truth.

Whilst he busied himself about the room I sat and meditated upon this mystery, before arriving at the solution in a sudden flash of deductive reasoning.

---

* See journal entry for 12th December 1905 on p.109.

At the moment I fell asleep the night before, Simpkins had been uninjured and in his usual position, seated at his desk at the foot of my bed and with his chin resting in his left hand to ease his posture throughout the night-long vigil. This is a key point. Deductive reasoning suggested to me that at some point during the night he had allowed himself to doze off, and in so doing had slipped from his supporting hand and fallen forward onto the burning stump of candle that illuminates his desk. Quite obviously, given the nature of his injuries, the stump had struck him very squarely in the left eye socket, the twin collisions with the burning wick and the surrounding crater of molten wax both being contributors to the inflammation of the skin, the crustiness of the lids, the corneal damage, and the dozens of tiny blisters discernible on the surface of the eye itself. Upon close inspection it was even possible to make out small blobs of wax adhering to his eyelashes and eyebrows, although he had clearly done his best throughout the night to divest himself of such incriminating evidence.

Protocol dictated that I should punish him immediately for his delinquency, but I pride myself on knowing when understanding will prove a better master than the rod when dealing with servants; and moreover I reasoned that justice was at least partially satisfied by the fact that he had already suffered extensive personal injury by his own carelessness. Accordingly, I gave him a cursory examination, consoled him with the news that he may regain partial sight in the eye, and then sent him to Cook so that she might apply beaten egg whites to the site of the injury (meringue being an excellent cure for inflammation), instructing him to lie prone on the kitchen floor while she applied the soothing mixture liberally with a basting spoon.

I arose from bed a few minutes later feeling very elated, for there is little like mental exercise to stimulate one at the beginning of the day. The episode only added to an existing sense of well-being on that particular morning because I was already anticipating the pleasure of entertaining to afternoon tea a lady to whom discretion requires the application of an incognito. I shall refer to her as 'Miss X' when transcribing later events.* Suffice it to say, though, that I had every hope that the day would conclude with her acceptance of my proposal that we should marry!

Accordingly, with an air of enthusiasm I do not often allow myself to display in the presence of domestic staff, I allowed Fairbanks to invigorate my legs with a rough towel, dress me, and

(Three hundred and twenty-two pages here omitted. Ed.*)*

pointing out to her that it was not without risk, but at no time did she seem to object, simply moving her head back and forth to avoid the missile as though it were a shuttlecock. I was tempted to intervene and remonstrate with them, but forsook the notion when I saw that they meant her no direct harm and instead concentrated my efforts on trying to explain to Cook that the cake must be more moist throughout, and that the cucumber in the sandwiches must be sliced more thinly to reduce the possibility of flatulence in those keen to avoid it.

Typically, she was both aggressive and adamant** in her denials, stating emphatically that the cucumber slices she prepares are always 'wafer thin'. But the truth is that her eyesight is no longer as acute as it once was and her cucumber 'slices' are often over an inch§ thick, producing sandwiches of such magnitude that it is a significant challenge to insert one even into a mouth opened at full stretch. However, pride would not allow her to countenance my assertions, so instead I took Grafton to one side and bade him

---

* The lady in question was almost certainly Miss Lallia Patterson (see p.137).

** See pp.144-145 for another instance of Cook's stubbornness.

§ 25mm

remake the sandwiches covertly by re-slicing the contents to a gauge acceptable to guests of quality. In the interests of hygiene, as emphasised recently by Doublanche's work on microbes, I also bade him be sure to wash any grime remaining on his hands after coming in from the stables.

When I left the kitchen I glanced into the corner and could see that the boot boy was already recovering from his ordeal, having been assisted into an upright position by other kitchen staff who seemed less concerned now that the bleeding was starting to clot. I

(One hundred and ninety-eight pages here omitted. Ed.*)*

standing uncertainly, with an expression of no small bemusement on his face as it dripped unrelentingly, as though he expected the tarpaulin to cover *even* the arms. Many laughed in empathy, but Guscott was sarcastic with him, and spoke with him in an offhand fashion as if he were a coolie (for Guscott can be out of humour upon a whim), and bade him take it all away and then come back quickly to try to clean away the stains and remove the smell.

Throughout this I had sat silently, because I was hoping for an audience with Bulstrode in order to garner some advice in readiness for the arrival of Miss X later in the day. I have little social experience with women, whereas Bulstrode is regarded widely as a satyr and so I felt confident that he would have something of value to impart.

We met finally at the buffet table, the enormous log-like stumps of his legs a very obvious burden to him as they moved him slowly and ponderously through the crowd in search of more food. When he was finally at rest, I laid my situation before him for appraisal, but the bulk of his advice was of no value since it referred to various physical matters connected to post-matrimonial activities rather than to verbal exchanges prior to congress. Therefore it would have been as well if I had saved my efforts and left earlier, while lunchtime proceedings were suspended during the removal of Devenish. To effect my egress undetected I elected to wait patiently, knowing that it could not be overlong before Norbetton-Pump required medical attention due to the nervous alacrity with which he was talking loudly in an almost continuous expostulation. I had seen him do it before and knew that it could not last, for there is not energy enough in the human body to sustain it. I was proven right some ten minutes later when he collapsed suddenly in mid-sentence, his head actually breaking the heavy dinner-plate onto which it fell. The fellow next to him was thoughtful enough to turn his face to the side to ensure that his airways would not become blocked by gravy. I reflected to myself that it would be a dreadful irony for any man to be drowned so ignominiously in his own food – the more so in Norbetton-Pump's case, since Lady Norbetton-Pump would certainly become furious. A furious Lady Norbetton-Pump is a frightening prospect for any man because of her weight.

As his aides rushed in to revive him, I left the premises undetected and travelled home by cab. On the journey I reflected that no matter how many human beings are crammed into small accommodations within London, many in conditions of the utmost squalor

(Four hundred and six pages here omitted. Ed.*)*

throughout the entire ritual that was often observed at dusk, provided he had dressed himself for the occasion in the correct habiliments. No one moved, although there was a gasp of admiration as he used a shaped piece of wire to make a small scalloped pattern on the edges.

I then saw Father press his thumb discreetly against the slice of cake as it was passed to her, doubtless to check its moisture content against his own in order to assess whether baking had been even throughout the whole cake. Miss X took it with good grace, even though I suspect she witnessed the touch of his thumb, and placed the cake beside the cucumber sandwich that had caused her such difficulties some five minutes earlier.

There was an embarrassed pause while no one could think of anything to say, but then after several minutes of general silence Miss X intervened and offered to amuse everyone with an imitation of birdsong taught to her by her father. This interruption covered the awkwardness wonderfully, even though no one accepted the offer, and we were soon able to pass on to other things.

Julius* regaled us for seven minutes and twenty-eight seconds with an amusing story about a lighthouse, but it was beyond the comprehension of most of us for it was couched in some form of dialectical patois relevant to the subject matter. Therefore its conclusion was met with complete silence and considerable disapproval from Father, causing Jaliska** to suddenly emit a high-pitched hysterical laugh in a loyal attempt to cover his *faux pas.* Father silenced her with an angry glance. It was another awkward moment and many elected to make a further assault on their sandwiches.

Suddenly, Miss X clapped her hands to attract attention and launched into a humorous anecdote about porpoises. Within seconds it had become so amusing that even those on the outer fringes of the gathering began moving closer to hear her.

I watched her in admiration as she spoke, and realised that she was both confident and relaxed in demeanour, the scrutiny of so many others notwithstanding. She was, in fact, simply the least rigid and most wonderful lady in whose company I had endeav-

---

* Jeremy's older brother

** Jaliska Hanna Lebowski, sister of the Polish trichologist Jan Lebowski who was researching a painless cure for psoriasis, married Julius in 1888. She suffered continual bowel trouble that eventually soured their relationship.

oured to pass time. But not *louche* or low! Rather, she was utterly charming, and there was an enviable easiness about her that betokened considerable past experience in company. As she sat beside me upon the ottoman she several times emphasized a point in her story by a brief touch of her fingers upon my knee or thigh, made lightly and deftly. I am sure that none of those present noticed, for it was done so quickly and her arms and hands were almost a blur of motion as her story reached its climax; but to me the moment was far from lost. Although I knew her touches to be innocent of intention and wholly inadvertent, done as they were without conscious thought on her part, they engendered something special within me – I know not what precisely – that caused me to experience feelings the like of which were strangers to me.

On two occasions I glanced at her and caught her eye, and she gave me a penetrating look of such frank admiration, yet underscored with a certain subtle femininity that only women are capable of exuding, that I began to suspect, even to hope, that her fleeting touches were not mere inadvertencies but rather secret communications intended to convey to me that she reciprocated my burgeoning feelings of fondness! For in truth I think I was becoming besotted with her heady presence, with the sound of her voice, with the rapid windmilling of her arms . . . even with the relative sizes of her head and body. Her story concluded to cautious laughter from the assembly, after Father had given a solitary nod to signal his approval of the content.

Someone at the back of the drawing room, possibly Jacob*, applauded briefly before being silenced. It was a happy moment of general relaxation, and several separate conversations began among the assembled throng. Once or twice Miss X smiled secretly at me, covering the moment with the movement of her fan, and I felt something inside me, almost like the bubbling of a fountain or an eruption within my heart, which suffused me

* Jeremy's older brother

with a warm glow as though I were blushing.

As we sat, separated only by inches, I sensed myself becoming slowly disconnected from the conversations in the room, able to concentrate less on matters external to me. I became excited by the appearance of new sensations within and was careful to commit each to memory as it occurred. I found that my breathing had become heavier and much hoarser, and felt sure that the intense glow in my face must mean that my countenance had reddened significantly. Even my scalp prickled, and I could feel small rivulets of perspiration trickling through my hair. The heat in my face was unprecedented and I raised my hand to my cheek and was amazed by its intensity, discernable from a distance of over three inches.*

In addition I noted changes happening elsewhere. The majority of these were benign: a modest trembling in calf and thigh muscles, small pulsations of the pedal adductor muscles, and a moderate pulsing of the spinal erector muscles which caused me to rock back and forth slightly. But amidst all these sensations one jostled for supremacy for I was suddenly aware, to my complete horror and distress, that I was beginning to tumesce. To add to my discomfiture, it seemed that it was happening of its own accord, for I was wholly powerless to prevent it! It was not my first tumescence during daylight, but it *was* my first in proximity to a lady.

My first impulse was concealment. I was holding my side plate on my lap and endeavoured to slide it into a position that would obscure my revolting condition from the gaze of anyone close by. To assess the extent of the problem I then inclined the side plate very slowly and slightly, glanced down as surreptitiously as I could, and was horrified to see that the tumescence was extending along my thigh into a size and condition that would be quite evident to any onlooker should the side plate be removed. I lowered the plate to conceal it once more.

---

* c. 75mm

I had hoped for my subtle movements to go undetected, but Miss X was obviously a woman with great sensitivity and she looked at me in alarm. Her eyes filled with tender concern the moment she took in my perspiring and suffused countenance, her face softening as she observed the various tics that afflicted my face and upper body. However, as her gaze travelled down my torso I thought that I detected a very slight change in her expression, and I followed the direction of her glance with curiosity only to discover to my absolute horror that my tilted plate was obscuring my tumescence from the purview of *everyone in the room but Miss X* seated beside me!

The reader will understand at once that prose is unequal to the task of describing the self-loathing that engulfed me at this realisation: for to sit beside a lady of charm and expose her to the revolting sight of a pulsating tumescence is the act of a person of the lowest morals imaginable.

My first impulse was to rock the plate quickly to the right so that I might shield her eyes from the loathsome sight, but I was in a quandary inasmuch as the tumescence was acting as a fulcrum, and to tilt the plate to the right would necessitate lifting the left side of it, thereby exposing the tumescence to my father. I had no desire whatever for Miss X to witness his reaction should he take note of it.

I hovered in an agony of indecision for several seconds, the mobility of my facial features doubtless betraying the turmoil within, until Miss X attempted to come to my emotional rescue by raising her fan to cover her mouth and making a *moue* at my attempts to adjust the position of my plate. She then granted me the smallest of smiles, informing me by that small sign of Christian charity that she forgave me my incontinence and with it any offence I had caused her!

I could have wept with gratitude. The relief I experienced within was enormous, and I think it was at that moment that my heart cracked and overflowed with loving appreciation, for if she could face such a repellent display with poise and equanimity when it was thrust before her in so cavalier a manner then I reasoned that she was probably resilient enough to be induced into congress without hysteria. Yet even as I contemplated the degrading experiences to which such physical congress would subject her, I began to hate myself afresh for the agony she would endure in the name of procreation.

Meanwhile, in the room the general conversation quietened as Father began to lambast Gladstone, the Liberal party, the Dublin Irish, all Ulstermen, the French, Lowland Scots, Irving's funeral service*, pederasts, steam, and the morality of the Anglican clergy in a continuous tirade. As he moved steadily from one subject to the next I endeavoured to concentrate on his words in the hope that my tumescence would subside before Mother forced me to reveal it by offering another slice of cake.

I glanced at Miss X again, but found her gaze not on Father but on me. Her eyes seemed positively to bore into mine with a strange intensity I could not interpret. She then held fast to my gaze whilst lowering her fan very slowly to cover the small gap between our knees. I was at a momentary *non-plus* at her actions, one that only increased when she reached out her fingers under cover of the fan and allowed her gentle fingertips to begin tracing their way along my thigh *towards my tumescence...*!

I followed the movement with an understandable sense of confusion, unable to discern her purpose. So intent was my observation that I could feel my eyes bulge markedly as they tracked the agonisingly slow progress of her fingers along my leg.

Having started at my knee, she was soon within inches of the tumescence itself and I was without conception as to how to

* Sir Henry Irving, famous Shakespearean actor, palaeontologist and ethnobotanist, had died on the 13th October 1905. Josiah Selman-Troytt attended the funeral under duress and left noisily and publicly after the first eulogy.

proceed. I was held hostage to a double handicap: not only was her touch without precedent, but I had no idea how I was supposed to respond if her fingertips should inadvertently encounter my tumescence! Should I jerk away? Cough? Perhaps try to trap her fingers beneath my plate? The simple truth is that I had no idea of appropriate protocol in the circumstances and could only sit frozen, awaiting the moment of contact as her fingertips approached to within a hair's breadth. I began to feel waves of panic rise within me.

However, to my profound relief and great good fortune, the crisis was suddenly averted at the final moment by an involuntary process that took place within my own body. For at that precise instant I was lucky enough to suffer an ejaculation so powerful that the explosive force distended, and then rippled, the taut cloth of my right trouser leg. The physical law of reaction ensured that the emission was accompanied by a small but painful recoil in my lower torso, one whose force caused me to utter a low groan as I was forced backwards. The combination of movement and sound alerted Miss X to the fact that something had occurred, for there was an immediate halt in the advance of her fingertips. They remained hovering tentatively *in situ* for a few seconds, a mere fraction of an inch from the tumescence itself, whilst her eyes drank in the full particulars of the slowly darkening area to the fore of the bulge. Then her fingers began a slow retreat and were finally withdrawn into her own lap under cover of her fan.

When I glanced next at her face it was to see her features fully composed as she paid close attention to Father's disparaging opinion of Lord Acton's Catholicism. I searched in vain for some hint as to her feelings or opinions concerning my involuntary tumescence and abrupt ejaculation, but found none beyond a certain set to her mouth which suggested that she had experienced less revulsion than I had feared. Furthermore she appeared less confused than *I* felt, for matters were simply moving too fast for me to assimilate.

Meanwhile it should not be inferred that my involuntary emission, fortuitous though it was in saving me from the embarrassment of her touch, represented an immediate end to my problems. For not only had I ejaculated without permission in the presence of the very woman to whom I hoped shortly to propose, and not only was I forced to undergo the repellent experience of having seminal discharge in contact with my skin, but my breeches now bore very ample evidence of my recent transgression. Indeed, in some respects my predicament had worsened, for leaving the room undiscovered would now be fraught with difficulties. Not for the first time in my life I questioned the advisability of always wearing fawn-coloured trousers, for I think there is not a colour in the world that discloses a stain more readily!

I contemplated making my egress with the stain concealed behind a side plate pressed artfully to my thigh, but reasoned that all present in the room would consider it suspicious if I attempted to walk out with a plate held in so unorthodox a position.

I sat considering other solutions, all the while frustrated by my lack of ruler, callipers or pipette; for without them I was unable to measure either the dimensions of the stain itself or the quantity of ejaculate expelled. However, as so often happens to me in such moments of desperation, I was lifted in spirits by a sudden inspiration. Hitherto, I had been considering ways of removing or concealing the stain, but in a flash of insight I saw that my salvation lay in enlarging and worsening it!

I reasoned that all I had to do was feign clumsiness by tipping the contents of a teacup on to my thigh in order to give myself a perfect method of concealment, as well as a legitimate reason for excusing myself from the room. Once within the precincts of my own chambers I could then have Fairbanks change my clothing.

Immediately I signalled a footman for more tea which he presented to me with a bow. With my left hand I took careful delivery of the cup and saucer while still holding fast to my side plate with my right. Then, in a feat of prestidigitation of which

Maskelyne* would have been proud, I removed the side plate quickly with my right hand whilst apparently fumbling with my left and allowing the tea to cascade on to my lap and thigh. There was a collective gasp as those assembled witnessed my 'accident'.

I was absolutely elated, although my delight at the success of the operation was mitigated in part by the very high temperature of the tea that soaked through my trousers and scalded my thigh and my diminishing tumescence. Both injuries caused me intense pain, and I recorded mentally the necessity of having Fairbanks apply a soothing balm to them later.

In the silence that followed the incident I turned towards Father, apologised for my ineptitude, and begged to be allowed to leave the room while I attended to my toilet away from the public gaze.

Father gave his assent in a measured way and I stood, apologising profusely to everyone there for my gaucheness, and was about to step towards the door when I was arrested in mid-movement by Father, who barked that I should hold my place a moment.

I stood frozen as his gaze raked intently over my stained trousers. Suddenly his mouth set as he pointed an index finger slowly at my nether parts. I looked down in consternation, fearing myself undone, and discovered that, far from concealing the stain, the addition of hot liquid to the area had served to leach the salts from the seminal discharge, turning the original offending patch considerably lighter than its surroundings. At that instant I knew that all was lost.

---

* John Nevil Maskelyne (1839–1917) was a famous British stage magician and inventor. He invented the lock for cubicle doors which could be opened with penny coins in public toilets, giving rise to the Victorian euphemism 'to spend a penny'. The invention made him a millionaire. Ironically, the debonair Maskelyne refused to carry copper coinage with him in case its weight ruined the hang of his tailored lounge suits, and therefore often soiled himself during emergency visits to public lavatories for want of the means to gain entry to the cubicles.

Father's eyes travelled upwards and found mine. I burned with shame at the censure in his look. He searched my face interrogatively for a few seconds, before transferring his gaze to Miss X and then back to me. He oscillated between us several times, a contemplative expression flitting over his features as he studied her demure countenance. Then, leaning towards her in a very deliberate manner, he asked in tones that carried to all in the room: 'Did you make my son ejaculate?'

It was another awkward moment. I glanced nervously at Miss X, wanting to know how she would respond to the unwarranted accusation that she had been in some way responsible for my unexpected emission. However, far from being cowed by it, she was magnificent in her reaction. She sat up straighter upon the ottoman and looked directly at Father with defiance as she answered clearly in the negative.

I could tell that Father was far from satisfied with her denial, but he was powerless to do much beyond staring angrily at her for a few more seconds before bidding her to leave immediately. I found myself in an immediate quandary, for if she left without delay then I would miss the opportunity to propose to her, assuming that Father were still willing to give his assent to the match. I was tempted to ask her to wait in the library whilst I discussed matters with him, but the moment did not seem propitious. Instead, I decided that it would be better to allow her to take her leave unhindered, and then to inform her by letter whether her application had been successful.

She gathered her few things with great dignity, and then swept from the room imperiously. Her departure caused a small susurration in the room where Father, obviously now out of humour, announced that tea was cancelled as the moment had been spoiled. He looked directly at me with an accusatory stare when making this declaration.

He then summoned Fairbanks from the side of the room and informed him that he wanted my trousers, dried in readiness for inspection, brought to him within the hour. I had a brief moment of hope when I realised that I was to be left in the hands of our old retainer, but it was dashed when Father ordered Jonathan* to accompany us as an impartial witness so that he could ensure the trousers suffered no interference prior to Father's examination of them.

In due course the trousers were delivered to Father in order that he could satisfy himself that they were contaminated with ejaculate. His later confirmation of this fact set in motion other events, not all of which were of a positive nature insofar as their effects on me were concerned. However they are of a personal and private nature so I will exclude them from this account.

That concludes the circumstances in which I suffered my first involuntary ejaculation. As stated in my introduction, I have given considerable thought as to which factors may validly be described as 'contributory' and I am now in a position to postulate causality in certain of the links. This research will be published in a companion work, although the technical nature of it will render it less penetrable, and therefore less readable, to the non-scientist. Enquiries regarding this work should be made to my publisher.

J. S-T. 1906

* Jeremy's older brother

Romance

Lallia Patterson

Lallia Patterson was investigated thoroughly by the Selman-Troytt family immediately after she was suspected of causing Jeremy to ejaculate involuntarily.

After extensive research, investigators were able to confirm that she was not, as she had claimed, the only daughter of a remote Cornish vicar who had been swept out to sea while attempting to bless a new dory, but rather an enterprising young lady with a shady past and a growing reputation as a fortune hunter among the aging *parvenus* of London society.

Born Doreen Baaaals in Hackney, London, she had drifted into the murky world of illicit photography at the age of only thirteen. An attractive girl whose physical maturity had outpaced her years, she was offered work as a photographic model for a range of 'artistic illustrative postcards'. Initially, the photographs were innocent, with Doreen posed chastely and fully-clad adjacent to a bowl of fruit. However, they became more pornographic by degrees as the photographer gradually removed more of her clothing and moved her closer and closer to a banana.

The resulting collection was sold covertly on the streets of Paris as a series entitled 'Lallia Baise le Fruit'* and was an immediate success

* A modern yet sensitive translation of this might be *Lallia 'Does' Fruit.*

with all Frenchmen. As 'Lallia's' fame spread, Doreen Baaaals effectively ceased to exist.

By age eighteen Lallia had made the move from fruits and vegetables to penetrative sex and was often partnered by Dom 'The Gent' Pasternak (shown overleaf, with Lallia), a genteel Polish émigré with enormous genitals. She learned much from him, including the affectation of good manners and elocution, and heeded his advice that the fastest way out of the seedy world of pornography was to ensnare a rich man. Pasternak himself was engaged in the same pursuit and was at that time making considerable headway with Lord Northbury.

When photographic evidence of Lallia's past indiscretions was placed before a distraught Jeremy it was two days before he was able to take up his journal again.*

* Henceforth, the journals maintain an expressive silence with regard to Lallia and she is never mentioned again. However, some continuing emotional turmoil within Selman-Troytt must be inferred from the fact that his search for a spouse seems to have been suspended for a full year, while his journals record no further emissions or ejaculations for nearly fourteen months.

JOURNAL NOTES FOR JANUARY 17TH, 1907

Pederson attempts levity in his letters and fails! He has not my ability to combine occasional levity with gravitas to produce prose that is at once instructive and readable. He tries, but overreaches, often using absurdly elaborate phrases or attempting (but failing to find!) humorous asides. To me his method is transparent and vapid. I am sure others see through it also.

I hope for news of Miss Harrington. I am optimistic of a favourable response to my entreaties.

JOURNAL NOTES FOR JANUARY 22ND, 1907

Furious with Cartwright! Absolutely furious! Angered beyond words. How dare he question my judgement in front of others! The man knows nothing about haemoglobin. I would be amazed if he had read anything beyond an illustrated newspaper!

JOURNAL NOTES FOR JANUARY 23RD, 1907

Calmer today, but still unsettled. What gall! What effrontery! I am sure no other man would have been so brazen. Even now to dwell upon it reawakens the clamour within my brain! I shall consider my reply.

Too much pastry on the veal pie again! The walls were over two inches thick and it was a challenge to breach them to access the veal. I became exhausted before I had reached the meat. I have spoken to Cook about it but she repeats the same old excuse that her eyesight is failing and she can no longer judge thicknesses well. Whatever the truth of the matter, it is apparent that something is wrong as her pies are becoming much thicker and heavier, each one containing extraordinary quantities of pastry, such that the weight of a single slice can prove too much for an ordinary china plate. I may have to consider allocating an assistant to guide her hands and inform her of thicknesses.

Journal notes for February 20th, 1907

Rokeby called about the dust (nearly two years late!). He cited logistical difficulties in organising the journey here, despite living only two hundred paces away on the opposite side of the Square. At any rate, he echoed my own concerns with regard to dust: he says there *is* a lot, at least in his unprofessional opinion as a layman with no particular expertise in dust or cleaning. In his preliminary judgement – he will not commit to a final judgement without further research – a professional appraisal should be sought re dust. I have told him I will sleep on it.

Journal notes for March 3rd, 1907

I am encouraged by the responses of Miss Evesham, who writes that she does not find my advances wholly unwelcome. She comments a little upon my shape, which is to be expected, but says I may call upon her nevertheless provided I wear a retainer. I find my spirits lightened. I shall consider an appropriate present. Guscott says this should not be money or food.

JOURNAL NOTES FOR MAY 5TH, 1908

Monthly examination of Jonty.* Stools moist and sputum clear, but I expressed concern at the condition of his genitals (peeling and swollen). However he brushed aside my comments with contempt and left angrily without speaking.

JOURNAL NOTES FOR SEPTEMBER 4TH, 1908

Letters of support come in following publication of *FBTB*.** Most pleasing.

An interesting event occurred after luncheon. I thought I had a moment of self doubt, which passed very quickly and left me quite shaken at its appearance. When I examined it later I realised that it was not self-doubt at all – thanks be to the Almighty! – but rather a small intestinal tremor. I am not sure what I would do if I were afflicted with self-doubt.

* Jeremy's older brother

** *From Bite to Bolus – 1202 Detailed Observations of Mastication & Swallowing*, O'Rourke & LeFevre, London, 1908

PART THREE

The Sexual Years

1909–1916

JOURNAL NOTES FOR FEBRUARY 14TH, 1909

I have received a greeting card of some kind with a question mark written upon it. Most perplexing. Viewed under a powerful magnifying glass, the writing looks familiar. It could belong to either Cholpley or Paving. Beneath the question mark is the inscription: 'I yearn for you with pumping heat', which makes no sense at all. Orthographical error? 'Heart' perhaps? Even then it makes no sense. I shall speak to Cholpley about this. How dare my time be wasted this way!

JOURNAL NOTES FOR FEBRUARY 15TH, 1909

Another letter threatening me with death. It cannot be from the same person as last time because the signatures are different. I am still using Simpkins as a decoy. Every night he circles the house while dressed in my coat and hat, but I am losing confidence in his effectiveness. Thus far he has yet to be approached by anyone, not even to speak, let alone be assaulted. I wonder if his rolling gait and diminutive stature are acting as deterrents? I will experiment by increasing the frequency of his circumambulations.

JOURNAL NOTES FOR JUNE 30TH, 1909

Annual discussion with cook regarding change to household brand of meat paste. The foolish woman cannot see that I am obdurate and will never yield to her on this point. I suspect that she will continue to raise it annually until one of us dies! Be that as it may, I determined many years ago that she will never win this point. It is a matter of principle. I know this because I dislike the brand of paste we have been using for the last ten years, and actually *prefer* the brand she is proposing – a fact I have stressed to her in order to attest to the purity of my intentions in denying her request! Yet still she adds the item to the agenda. Does the woman not understand that, if I allow this change, then other changes could be precipitated?

Journal notes for July 6th, 1909

Another card, this time a postcard with crudely drawn genitalia on it. I am unsure if it is from a detractor or a prospective patient. I am unable to identify the sender, as it is unsigned and the genitals do not look familiar, even under a microscope.

I have just realised that 'detractor' rhymes with 'retractor'. Could this be used in future commercial promotion, in some way? I shall file this thought away for future study.

Journal Notes for September 8th, 1909

Aunt Jennifer called to take tea and to assess my progress with the lotion I promised her in 1885. Her desquamation seems to have worsened, and as she shuffled slowly along the hall she left two trails behind her that looked for all the world like ridged trails of small snowflakes. Millie was forced to follow her, crouching behind her and moving crabwise as she swept the debris directly into a dustpan before stray breezes could take it and distribute it about the house and onto our foodstuffs.

A bill from Sedge & Frowse. I am tempted to pay them, since the account they enclose is accurate, and the goods arrived on time and in perfect condition.

Contemporaries

Jefferson Lemurre

Mr. Lemurre (above, leading the camel), shown in native dress during a final date-buying expedition through North Africa with Garson Hennessy, father of Jeremy's friend Charles.

Lemurre's appetite was legendary, and he kept a knife and fork on a lanyard around his neck so that, as he put it, '*I can always lay hands on my eating irons in any emergency.*' He is rumoured to have once devoured several goats during a two-day eating frenzy in Boulogne.

What is not rumour is that on 8th October 1914 Mr. Lemurre agreed to drink the entire window display of *Morgan's Ale Shop* (right) for a bet. Alas, this was to prove too much even for '*The Omnivore*', as he was fondly nicknamed, and he was admitted to St. Bartholomew Hospital, London where he managed a final goose before his liver exploded.

Speculations Upon Improbable Joint Articulations

BEING THE AUTHOR'S SPECULATIONS UPON THE WAY JOINTS MIGHT BE ARTICULATED UNDER CONDITIONS DIFFERENT FROM THOSE WHICH CURRENTLY PERTAIN WITH REGARD TO THE HUMAN FORM

BY

JEREMY SELMAN-TROYTT

O'Rourke & LeFevre
London
MCMIX

Foreword

Speculations upon Improbable Joint Articulations (*SUIJA*) caused a sensation when it was published in 1909, principally because it exposed its readership to the possibility of joint articulations they had never even imagined, let alone seen.

It quickly became a bestseller, fuelling rumours that Selman-Troytt was about to pioneer ground-breaking surgery to experiment with some of the articulations depicted. In the event, these rumours proved to be unfounded, although Selman-Troytt certainly did experiment with joint design in the prostheses he made thereafter. For example, in the ivory legs he made for the Bishop of Exeter (British Museum ref: FG/ST62883-exeterlegs – 3/27) he moved away from the rigid, curved leg design he had employed hitherto* and inserted a ball-and-socket joint at the position of the knee, allowing the lower half of the legs complete freedom to move through 360 degrees in the horizontal plane and 270 degrees in the vertical. This gave the Bishop of Exeter extraordinary mobility, allowing him to fall in any direction without warning. Knowing that the legs could collapse in any direction, the Bishop countered this tendency by carrying himself forwards very slowly on strong crutches held under his armpits. For additional security, he had each leg moved forward manually and then held firmly in place by a verger whose responsibility it was to ensure that the lower halves remained vertical and stable enough to support the Bishop as he swung his crutches forward.

---

* See for example sailor's prostheses described on p.93.

In the first published edition of *SUIJA*, the illustrations were by von Knabel, the artist famous for caricaturing Lenin relentlessly until his sudden death after a fall from his studio window, but the following entries from Selman-Troytt's papers show some of Jeremy's original illustrations, upon which von Knabel's were based.

SUIJA mss – first folio – addenda 1/45c (Title: 'additional positions', p. 122)

BELOW IS AN ORIGINAL ILLUSTRATION by von Knabel of the prototype designs for the 'Exeter legs'. Note ball and socket joint innovation connecting 'thigh' to lower leg.

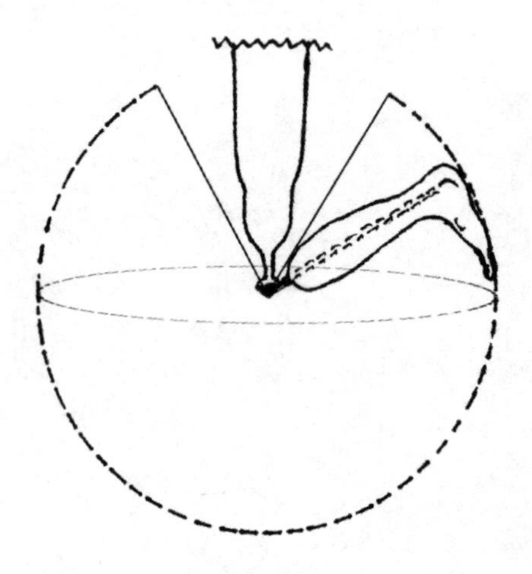

Fig. 16a: Exeter - Left Leg - Side View

Contemporaries

Geoffrey Harrington-Shine

First son of Hartley Harrington-Shine, the renowned expert on crustaceans, and heir to the Harrington-Shine hair tonic empire (*'Hairol – A Small Dab Banishes Baldness Forever!'*), Geoffrey was popular with those members of the London 'fast set' who, like him, were loud, brash, arrogant and aggressive. Always eager to prove himself in front of others, he once set fire to a waiter at Cowes *'just to prove it could be done'*.

His gambling addiction brought him into contact with many sporting heroes of the day, including C. B. Fry (overleaf), the famous cricketer and all-round athlete.

Their first notable meeting was at Selman-Troytt's home where the multi-talented Fry – with customary confidence and panache – revealed to the young bucks gathered there that he was capable of positioning himself in front of the library fireplace and then jumping backwards up onto the mantelpiece. The athletic Fry then proceeded to demonstrate this feat to the astonishment of an appreciative crowd that cheered him to the rafters.

Insecure enough to be bothered when another stole the limelight, and boastful and impulsive by nature, Harrington-Shine then pushed himself forward and denounced Fry's achievement as *'a mere child's trick'* that meant nothing when *'lifting only one's body'*. He went on to assert that *'A real man could do it carrying a very heavy weight!'*

So saying, he snatched up a nearby coal scuttle containing some 45 lbs (c. 20kg) of coal, hugged it to his chest, and then launched himself up and backwards towards the mantelpiece, from which a startled Fry stared down in consternation.

Unfortunately for Harrington-Shine, a combination of lesser thigh power and greater body mass conspired to send him in a much lower trajectory than Fry's, such that he missed the mantelpiece completely and sailed head first into the flaming coals of the fireplace, setting his frock coat alight and inflicting such burns to the head that his hair subsequently grew back in unsightly clumps that not even Hairol could eradicate.

For the rest of his life he held Fry responsible for his disfigurement, and pursued him remorselessly in public, often baiting him beyond endurance. When Fry later suffered a nervous breakdown, one symptom of which was a paranoid fear of Indians, Harrington-Shine would frequently darken his skin with a mixture of animal fat and cocoa powder and then leap out on Fry from various places of concealment, hoping to provoke a coronary.

The Deluge Patent Whirlpool Cistern:
"One pull scours your U-bend!"

The deleterious effect of this upon Fry was noticeable. He became increasingly nervous and unreliable, often refusing to travel anywhere unless the route had been pre-checked for Indians. His income from celebrity appearances and endorsements began to suffer as offers slowly declined. Whereas once he had enjoyed considerable wealth from endorsing the very best quality cricket equipment, he ended his days advertising a range of less glamorous items such as surgical trusses and sanitary ware.

Journal notes for May 9th, 1910

I observe an interesting change happening within my practice. Increasingly I find myself counselling patients regarding matters connected with various problems within their marital relationships. Although such consultations were not unknown before, they have increased markedly since the publication of *FSTS*.* I did anticipate the public clamour for the book, but not this effect.

Journal notes for May 11th, 1910

More appointments made today to consult over matrimonial matters.

This new advisory role is one with which I believe I will find myself more and more comfortable, for as a scientist I am able to discuss anatomical matters objectively, thereby relieving any embarrassment that may attend such meetings were they presided over by a lay-person. For example, I am able stare at the private parts quite dispassionately, having trained myself to overcome the natural impulse to avert one's eyes.

I am discommoded only when parts are exposed suddenly and without warning, the more so when they are a woman's parts, for it is difficult to conceive of a woman other than in a context where she is behaving gently and where her modesty is covered completely. Therefore to find her parts suddenly exposed can be

* *From Salve to Splint – Curing Erectile Dysfunction*, O'Rourke & LeFevre, London.

nerve-racking. I have observed to my surprise that women are considerably more aggressive in this regard, requiring no prompting to expose a breast or *mons veneris* and thrust it close to my eyes for my opinion as to whether a husband or suitor may find it attractive. (Men, by contrast, can be reticent in the extreme, and may even need to have their parts exposed for them before any opinion can be rendered as to whether their prepuces are acceptable. This anomaly may be worthy of further analysis.)

If only I could learn *more* to improve my critical faculties. I should not wish to classify a prepuce erroneously, or to specify a *mons veneris* as attractive when it is not. Either mistake might generate a complaint. I have been pondering whether it is worthwhile to pay subjects in order to study a vast array of organs, so as to avoid all possibility of error...

Perhaps tomorrow I shall send Fairbanks to St. Pancras to establish whether poor women would be willing to expose their parts for payment. Sketches (or even photographs) could then be made and used during consultations. More thought required on this as I know photographic equipment to be bulky and unwieldy. Close work on the pudenda may require a platform of some kind. Discuss with Farnaby?

JOURNAL NOTES FOR MAY 11TH, 1910

Re: close study of sexual organs – could one take a cast of a lady's pudenda for further close examination at one's leisure? If so, might plaster of Paris be a suitable medium? Perhaps poured into a cardboard mould-ring placed around the *mons veneris* if the lady were inverted?

N.B. Mould-ring may cement itself to the pubis so prior depilation would be necessary to prevent adhesion. Corollary: casts of male genitals – adhesion to the prepuce?

JOURNAL NOTES FOR JUNE 2ND, 1910

Tailor arrived today for another trouser fitting but then said he had miscalculated (again!) and had not allowed for enough material in the thighs! A d_____ nuisance, since I long for replacements. He is sending to Islay for more tweed. He might as well send to Pago Pago for a cocoanut!

JOURNAL NOTES FOR AUGUST 24TH, 1910

McKindrick came to the *front* door and not the tradesmen's entrance for the *eleventh* time in a row. I know not what to do. He appears deaf to requests, entreaties and demands ... even threats. He seems wilfully non-compliant, almost as if to spite me. And there is about him an air of insolence. When I hear his thunderous knock upon the front door a dread passes through me. Is he mocking me?

There is more dust in the house than I remember.

Last post of the day has been delivered. Nothing from Stanleyson. Has he perhaps overlooked my correspondence in error? I know he is busy. I shall write to him again tomorrow.

J. SELMAN-TROYTT, ESQ.,
14 BERKELEY SQUARE, LONDON, W.

Lord Stainforth,
27 Piccadilly,
London, W.

19 February, 1911

Stainforth,

I have spent considerable time analysing your behaviour at dinner last night. I have reached no firm conclusion, as several possibilities present themselves. One is that you were trying to be amusing. Another is that you had difficulties with the pork because it was thinly sliced. Can you confirm which it was?

Selman-Troytt

P.S. My father was offended that you brought your own cutlery. We had cutlery for you.

Journal notes for April 17th, 1911

After so much recent discussion on the topic at the Athenaeum I find myself increasingly haunted by the unknown complexities of female genital construction. Am desperate to begin study, analysis and comparison of pudenda but constrained by circumstances and prohibited by lack of samples. Frustration unendurable! If only I had a wife! Can a substitute be found? Cook? Despite her weight and eyesight? Would Fairbanks agree? Milly? Sarah, if paid an extra shilling?

An odd day. Everything seemed to run backwards. Even time.

Journal notes for June 20th, 1911

Very constructive meeting with Cannonby about the retractor. I demonstrated a persistent problem with the rubber-tipped clamp, whereby the rubber, if tacky through insufficient curing, adheres aggressively to the glans. Cannonby tested it for himself and agreed it was very painful if pulled off sharply. He suggested various substitutes which I shall now try. He also suggested an improvement in the lubrication for the thrust bearing. Good old Cannonby! It is a comfort at times to have a colleague upon whom one can depend.

Journal notes for July 8th, 1911

Distressing news today from Henderson's. They cannot manufacture a lightweight casing with the strength required. According to their chief engineer, a casing with the strength necessary to support the pressure of the clamp activator will actually increase the weight of the retractor! I am despondent. It must be portable or all is lost!

Furthermore, the cantilever arm is still not sensitive enough. Movements too jerky, even with new soft-metal bearing and thinner grease. Very difficult to align clamp accurately with prepuce, and the frictional coefficients are still too variable, so that clamp pressure oscillates unpredictably between 1oz (28.3g) and 24lb (10.8kg). This is enough to crush the glans if misaligned! Users will lose faith if this happens. How did Rochemel do it? If only I had one of his original machines to study!

JOURNAL NOTES FOR AUGUST 27TH, 1911

There seems to be a lot of dust in the house. I have measured its thickness in several locations. It is variable. I should have been monitoring this. Now I have no past data from which to extrapolate theoretical hypotheses, so I feel unmoored. I may ask Rokeby for his opinion on the dust as I seem to recall that he has a reputation for expertise in that area.

Lichens not yet harvested. This is always the nerve-racking part of the process because a single slip can undo the work of a decade.

Induced rash on Fairbanks for next lotion test (sample reference: F3284C).

JOURNAL NOTES FOR NOVEMBER 7TH, 1911

I endeavour always to remain objective and detached in my work but there are times when circumstances compel compassion to disrupt my *sang froid*. Today's consultation with Lord Soames was such an occasion, for the man even cried in my presence. I tried to show kindness by lending him a handkerchief, but he returned it soiled so I had Fairbanks dispose of it. He apologised for his distress, stating that it was allied to extreme frustration. He explained his position as follows. He is 52 and has suffered with erectile dysfunction for some years. His last recorded tumescence was on September 6th, 1907 at five minutes past ten in the morning. However, not knowing it would be his last, he failed to do anything constructive with it and simply thought about neutral matters until it subsided. Unsurprisingly, he now berates himself for not having made proper use of it.

Since then he has been unable to penetrate Lady Soames, whom he adores. However he confided to me that he worries that she may have satisfied her own physical needs through affairs in the interim, because she has thrice been treated for gonorrhoea since 1908. Her ladyship is now twenty-four and is regarded by Lord Soames as a great beauty. He became emotional while describing the shape of her buttocks.

In an effort to overcome his dysfunction he has tried numerous remedies, including the old 'folk' remedy of ingesting garlic in very large quantities (up to nineteen bulbs a day). Apparently this has had a positive effect, producing a tumescence that he describes as 'absolutely bulging'. However, when he tried to make use of it with Lady Soames, she could not countenance his presence because of the overwhelming smell of the garlic, which made her nauseated. He therefore withdrew from her chambers and forewent the garlic for four days, by which time she could suffer him to come within coupling distance once more. Unfortunately by then the tumescence had subsided and he was unable to regain it. With the ingestion of more garlic it returned, but then his wife was compelled to keep him at a distance once more. And so this cycle continued for five months during which time he was unable to utilise his tumescences on Lady Soames, who relapsed frequently into hysteria.

The case is without precedent in my experience. I attempted to view the matter logically and saw that there were only two courses he could take: either to find a less offensive compound or reagent than the garlic, or to render Lady Soames unaffected by his smell. I have made three suggestions with regard to the latter: that he stop her nostrils with plugs (he was not sanguine that she would concur, for he relates that she is extremely vain and would become hysterical were her nostrils to be distended); that he place her head in a sealed bag (again, he feels her vanity would not countenance this); or that he encourage her to breathe the air of another environment whilst congress is effectuated.

It was the last of these that he considered carried the greatest chance of success, particularly when I was inspired to suggest that this could be accomplished without offence to her vanity by encouraging her to place her head out of the bedroom window while the penetration takes place from behind. Given the location of their London residence, this will necessitate bending her forwards over the window sill so that she is looking along Regent Street, and then lowering the window sash gently onto to her back. Lord Soames can then stand at the window as though searching the street for a friend, and the actual nature of their activity should not be obvious to anyone glancing up.

Lord Soames left a great deal cheered, almost giddy. He began eating a bulb of garlic even as he left. I was a good deal cheered myself, for it is always satisfying to help a patient, particularly one as eager and enthusiastic as His Lordship. I imagine an insertion is imminent.

Journal notes for November 9th, 1911

Ambivalent letter from Lord Soames. As predicted by him, Her Ladyship would not consent to nostril plugs or a head bag. Fortunately she was amenable to the window proposal and Lord Soames ingested the requisite quantity of garlic. However, when they tried the exercise she found the outside temperature too harsh, even when she was wrapped in furs, and called a halt to the exercise before Lord Soames could make the insertion. She says she will agree to another trial in the warmer spring weather but His Lordship is beside himself with frustration now. He begs me to find another solution that will grant him the insertion he desires, but as I write this my mind is blank.

Journal notes for November 14th, 1911

An inspiration! I have asked His Lordship to attend another consultation on 22nd November and have demanded that he ingest no garlic between now and then.

Journal notes for November 22nd, 1911

Extraordinary instance of serendipity with Lord Soames!

I recalled from notes taken on the 7th that before his current period of dysfunction, Lord Soames had been used to gaining his tumescences by the simple expedient of having Her Ladyship blow gently upon the shaft. Since then I have been seeking some method that might mimic the effect of Lady Soames blowing upon the shaft. When he arrived today I had several pieces of apparatus in readiness. I bade him lie upon the couch directly, with the shaft exposed, and I then proceeded to direct air at the shaft from a tube and nozzle, using a variety of angles, strengths, temperatures and concentrations – from a soft, diffused zephyr-like wafting of air to a fast, cold jet concentrated directed down onto the glans. These produced varying verbal responses, but the shaft itself remained unaffected.

My second approach was an attempt to surround the whole shaft with a moving current of warm air. One of the pieces of equipment I had ready was an Everson Column jar, which I reasoned was just long and wide enough to accommodate a tumescent shaft of normal proportions. My plan was to attach an air hose to the end valve and then gently introduce a stream of air into the glass column. I placed Lord Soames's shaft inside the Everson Column using tongs, then placed the column jar vertically with the base secured upon his pubic bone, which I had instructed Fairbanks to depilate whilst I polished and greased the rim of the Everson Column. I reasoned that providing an airtight seal at the base might create a modest air pressure inside the jar and I wanted to see whether this would have an effect upon his flaccidity.

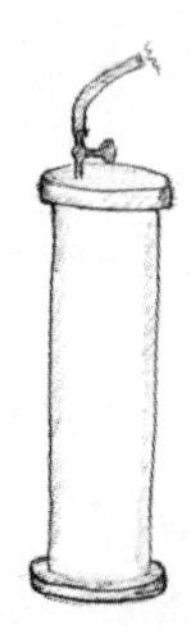

Everson Column Jar

What happened next was as exciting as it was serendipitous, for it was by pure accident alone that I connected the other end of the connecting air hose to the *inlet* valve of the air pump rather than to the *outlet* valve. Therefore, when the pump was switched on a *vacuum* was created inside the glass column and *not* a pressure. The effect was remarkable! Within seconds Lord Soames had grown extraordinarily tumescent and engorged, the shaft all but filling the interior of the Everson Column. His Lordship became enormously excited and shouted over the roar of the pump that it was the strongest tumescence he had ever had. He bade me bring him a tape measure so that he could record the length of the shaft in order to share the dimensions with Lady Soames.

Whilst he set about making his various measurements, I had Fairbanks make quick notes with accompanying sketches so as not to forget any of the steps that had led to this remarkable discovery. I was so excited that I could hardly keep my hands from dancing over the Everson Column. When the sketches were complete, Lord Soames bade me remove the column so that he could make measurements of the girth. He confided, as an aside, that he was somewhat apprehensive, for he had never known so significant a tumescence and knew not whether Lady Soames would be able to accommodate it.

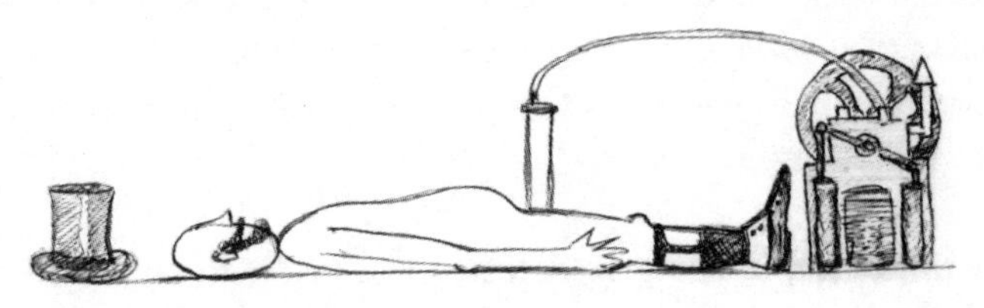

Lord Soames undergoing treatment - 22nd November 1911. Case reference: LS/32b - SD54W

I stopped the pump and released the vacuum inside the column, but even as I began to lift it a perceptible change had come over the shaft. It was noticeably less rigid and thickened. By the time the jar cleared the end of the glans there was already a discernible bend appearing. I was counting off the seconds mentally, using the military formula for approximating time ('One thousand and one searching sepoys, one thousand and two searching sepoys . . .'), and by that reckoning the shaft had reached a distinct parabola by six seconds, and was completely flaccid by thirteen. Lord Soames bade me replace the jar quickly and repeat the operation, which I did, and within seconds he was gasping and tumescent once more. But once again he became flaccid when the jar was removed. This time I had taken the precaution of having Simpkins stand by with a stop-watch and he was able to record the time from rigid tumescence to shrunken flaccidity at 12.3 seconds. Lord Soames's response was close to panic, and he shouted out that this was insufficient time in which to accomplish anything useful, especially as the rigidity necessary for initial penetration lasted less than 3.1 seconds. He was convinced that this was not enough time in which to penetrate Lady Soames, even if she could somehow hover suspended over the shaft as the Everson Column was whisked away.

I could tell Lord Soames was frustrated, from the way he slapped hard at his thighs and uttered a continuous string of oaths as he plucked at his own flesh. He became mollified and quietened only when the Everson Column was applied to the shaft and he was brought back to tumescence, but returned to physical and spiritual flaccidity as soon as it was removed. He bade me repeat this cycle more than a dozen times before I cried halt in the interests of safety and reason.

Loath as I am to admit to defeat, I had finally to break the news to him that there was nothing more to be done. I think it was a measure of his own desperation that he quickly suggested that perhaps Lady Soames could be induced to allow him to penetrate her whilst he was wearing the Everson Column. I explained that even if Lady Soames could accommodate the jar internally, and even if both parties were prepared to forego the touch of actual flesh upon flesh, there remained the insurmountable technical hurdle of how one might attach the vacuum hose to the upper end of the Everson Column that would be *inside* Her Ladyship.

His Lordship finally assented, but not with any grace, for he divested himself of the column roughly, cracking it in the process, and flung himself from the room in the blackest of moods and in a state of partial undress. It was as if his toilet had ceased to matter to him in this period of distraction.

The episode left me troubled in the extreme.

Journal notes for November 29th, 1911

Difficult meeting with Father today. I asked him to advance me a further £10,000 for continuing research on the retractor, but he began by mocking my rate of progress to date and then became abusive when I demurred. I explained yet again that producing a floor-standing version was much less demanding, and that it was pursuing the dream of making the contrivance portable that had absorbed so much time and money to date. I tried to be firm and convincing but Father generally takes only one idea into his head at a time (as he says frequently: 'one idea is enough for a lifetime'). I am desperate, and more dependent than ever on Father since Hennessy's suffocation. The money from my practice barely funds my lotion research, let alone my work on the retractor! Without Father's backing, the retractor may never be realised!

Journal notes for December 9th, 1911

Very interesting excursion to Royal Opera House* at the insistence of Lallap. Awkward beginning in foyer because Lemurre

* Sited in London's Covent Garden, the Royal Opera House began life as the Theatre Royal in the early 18th century. It staged many famous operas, including Rossini's *La Festa Di Carne* (The Meat Feast).

had bought a ham with him and argued with Kennett over whether it was concealed properly by the topcoat he carried over his arm for that purpose. Guscott was by turns apprehensive and animated because he had arranged for us to meet his latest fiancée, Miss Emma Cloth-Whickerby. He has regaled us with stories of her beauty these past three weeks and was beside himself with excitement at the prospect of impressing us with her presence.

When she arrived I believe we were all stunned completely. Guscott has always reserved his affections for women with a prognathous lower jaw, but Miss Cloth-Whickerby had the largest I have ever seen. I calculated that her lower jaw overshot her upper by nearly 3 inches (7.5cm), and when introductions were made Guscott could hardly contain his joy at our expressions of amazement. Miss Cloth-Whickerby did her best to join us in conversation, but we were all too chivalrous to address her directly for it was clear that speech was an activity that gave her anxiety. She exhibited similar discomposure when eating and drinking during the interval. Obviously no one in the company was sufficiently impolite to stare at her directly, but on the periphery of our vision we were able to note her embarrassment at her own awkward and unsuccessful attempts to drink from a champagne glass in a conventional way. Eventually, believing herself unobserved, she discreetly tipped the contents into her lower jaw, not unlike someone emptying a bucket into a sink.

I was intrigued and excited, for I believe she would make an excellent subject for facial reconstruction. Perhaps some kind of upper labial prosthesis? This would grant proportion to her face but may make her appear more simian. I shall contact her in confidence and invite her for a consultation.

Patients

Miss Emma Cloth-Whickerby

Miss Emma Cloth-Whickerby (left), Guscott's fiancée, and (below right) an artist's impression of how Selman-Troytt's proposed labial prosthesis might improve her appearance by '*rebalancing her face*'.

Miss Cloth-Whickerby was said to have wept with relief when she saw the proposed changes, but Guscott* forbade the treatment, fearing that it would change his feelings for her.

* See p.27.

Romance

Victoria Pershing

Victoria came only briefly into Jeremy's life, their affair overshadowed by his extensive correspondence with Stanleyson and his attempts to build a portable prepuce retractor.

Neither was attracted to the other physically, Victoria having often confided her concerns about his shape in notes she gave to her father. Jeremy wrote in his journal that he found her: '*strange in body and mind. A physical aberration. I would be convinced that she were mute if she did not speak.*'

Victoria did speak, but with a very unusual speech rhythm due to the fact that she never made an utterance until she had formulated and rehearsed each sentence thoroughly in her mind. This lent her discourse a staccato quality, with a rapid burst of speech followed by a very lengthy pause during which her face and eye movements betrayed the concentration happening within. Many interlocutors found this unnerving.

Victoria had only one accomplishment of note. In place of mastication she was able to use her throat muscles – strengthened by extensive practice in a life that contained few other diversions – to squeeze food under extreme pressure into a paste that could be pressed down her oesophagus. During this exercise her eyes would squeeze very tightly shut and her face become rigid and reddened as the pressure mounted. A slight rippling of her throat then marked the downward passage of the bolus. The operation complete, she would relax and proudly open her mouth to show that it was empty despite her jaws not having moved.

She gave two demonstrations to Jeremy, the first within a few seconds of their introduction to cover her nervousness. The second occurred a week later when Jeremy, once more in empirical mood, asked her to repeat the feat with some very dry pound cake he had had specially baked in an attempt to assess how she would fare with only limited saliva at her disposal.

J. SELMAN-TROYTT, ESQ.,
14 BERKELEY SQUARE, LONDON, W.

I. Selwyn-Trott, Esq.,
25 Bolsover Place,
London, W.

11 March, 1912

Dear Sir,

I thank you for your letter (with enclosures) of the 2 *inst*. The illustration that your wife chanced to see is the prototype design of a portable prepuce retractor. It was being returned to me by the engineering firm with which I am corresponding regarding its manufacture. If she experienced distress, as you say, then I apologise – although frankly I am surprised to learn of it, for if your marriage is a healthy one then your wife should have become very familiar with prepuces in the course of performing her wifely duties.

However, to the case in point. I concur with your suspicion that the fault lies with the local post office in mis-directing my correspondence to your address. Such an oversight is both incomprehensible and unforgivable. I have already written a stiff letter to them this morning, and shall send my butler to berate the manager in person unless I receive assurances that this will not occur again.

As to your other question: No, I have no recollection of receiving any of *your* correspondence, although it is always possible that letters of yours *were* delivered here but that my manservant destroyed them immediately when he noted they were not addressed to me.

If you receive any further correspondence addressed to me then I advise you to forward it here unopened to prevent further harm to your wife's sensibilities.

By way of compensation for the inconvenience that you have experienced I am prepared to offer you a consultation without charge in order to examine your prepuce (or that of any friend you nominate) in order to render my opinion upon it. The prepuce in question must be sanitised before presentation to me because I will not examine an offensive prepuce. Should you wish to avail yourself of this offer then please contact my assistant to make an appointment.

Your humble and obedient servant
J. Selman-Troytt

Journal notes for March 19th, 1912

Lenoir called today and asked me to change his dressings. I dread this, especially if it is close to breakfast time. Once the dressings were off I saw that they did not need changing, and reasoned that he had merely used them as an excuse to discuss a more confidential matter. I waited throughout the day, but when he seemed no closer to a revelation by mid-afternoon I became frustrated and had him put out.

Journal notes for April 15th, 1912

The Titanic has sunk and Willoughby-Gersh has been lost! An unimaginable tragedy, for he was carrying my follicle samples to Professor Montague for assessment. Newspapers report that nothing is recoverable from the sea. Ten years of collecting and cataloguing wasted! It is really too bad of Willoughby-Gersh, for he assured me that he was reliable. I shall now have to suffer the inconvenience of finding a replacement courier.

Romance

The Connaught Twins

A rare photograph of the Connaught twins, Elise and Litforth, making their first acquaintance with the matching cockatoos presented to them by Jeremy at their family home in Co. Meath, Ireland. Litforth's obvious nervousness is a testament to the ferocity and incontinence of the bird placed on her shoulder.

Lenoir, now confined to a bath chair, attended the presentation and had his physician remove his breathing tube so that he could proffer his congratulations.

By all accounts the afternoon passed well, with tea on the lawn and uproarious merriment had by all from Litforth's attempt to teach her bird a Gaelic sea-shanty. Even Lenoir laughed, despite knowing it could be fatal if his stitches opened.

That night saw Jeremy and Lenoir on the steam packet back to England. Both had very high hopes: Jeremy of receiving a *billet doux* from the girls; Lenoir of surviving the journey. However weeks passed without further word from either girl, and slowly Jeremy immersed himself in his work once more.

J. SELMAN-TROYTT, ESQ.,
14 BERKELEY SQUARE, LONDON, W.

Editor,
The Lancet,
c/o John Churchill,
46 Princes Street,
Leicester Square,
London, W.

3 August, 1912

Sir,

I write to take issue with the article entitled 'The Beneficial Effect of Daily Hardship upon Enhanced Brain Function – an examination of the relationship between environment and brain complexity', published in your most recent edition. I have never read such an absurd and fallacious article and I am surprised and chagrined that it should have passed moderation in so esteemed a publication as your own.

The author begins by asserting that intelligence increases the further north one travels from the Equator. This assertion is patently true, even to the non-scientific observer, and I have no quarrel with it. Who, for example, could argue that the Prussian is not both more intelligent and more industrious than the irrational, emotional and lethargic Italian? Or a Spaniard! The Latin is one thing, but the Teuton is quite another, in cerebral terms.

The premise is unarguable, but with the reasoning proposed to 'prove' it I must argue, forcibly. The author claims that the superior intelligence of the northern races is owing to the 'evolution' of the northern brain in response to more complex environmental factors.

My objection is thus: if the northern brain is 'evolving', and therefore growing larger than the southern brain, as he suggests, *then how should it continue to fit within our heads?* Common sense dictates that the brain must remain the same in size, or reach no more than a maximal size, for the cranial cavity is a container of finite volume and a growing brain would simply cease to fit within it. This much is obvious, for a continuously expanding brain would soon press our eyes out – yet even an untrained person may quickly discern that our eyes are not being pressed out!

No, while the author's premise is correct, his argument is nonsensical. I shall now offer the correct explanation.

We know, from study and mensuration, that the human body, and the human brain in particular, contains a high proportion of water. It is to this fact that we should direct our attention, for it bears heavily on the obvious reason for variations in intelligence, namely the relationship between water and temperature.

Consider for a moment the inner environment of the cranial cavity.

At higher temperatures the moisture inside the brain is evaporating, passing through the semi-permeable membrane of the 'sac' that encloses the brain and collecting inside the cranial cavity as a gaseous, steamy cloud around the now reduced and less moist brain. Inside its 'sac', the brain is drier, more compressed and altogether more lethargic. Now consider the analogy of an un-greased axle, with the wheel requiring more effort to turn on the dry 'bearing' surfaces. So it is with the brain, with thoughts requiring more effort to pass along the desiccated and constricted 'highways' within it.

However, at lower temperatures this vapour *condenses*, passing back through the covering of the 'sac' and re-hydrating the brain, which swells once more to a normal healthy size, becoming more moist and more lubricated as the 'sac' swells to fill almost all of the cranial cavity.

Thus it is that, in the northern hemisphere, a man may be made more intelligent and perspicacious by the simple expedient of transporting him north, and more sluggish and more idiotic simply by transporting him south. Indeed, how else would one propose to explain why the British Empire spans the globe while Bedouins are content merely to sit in a tent? It should be noted that this thermodynamic effect on intelligence is not instantaneous, since it requires a period of time for the moisture to pass through the dense membrane. However, simple observation will allow one to monitor the changes. For example, almost all Englishmen in the tropics succumb eventually to some kind of mental torpor, while, by contrast, Italians transported to Britain become more energised, more sober, less emotional, and more able to function in everyday commerce. Figure I shows the comparative effect of temperature upon the brain.

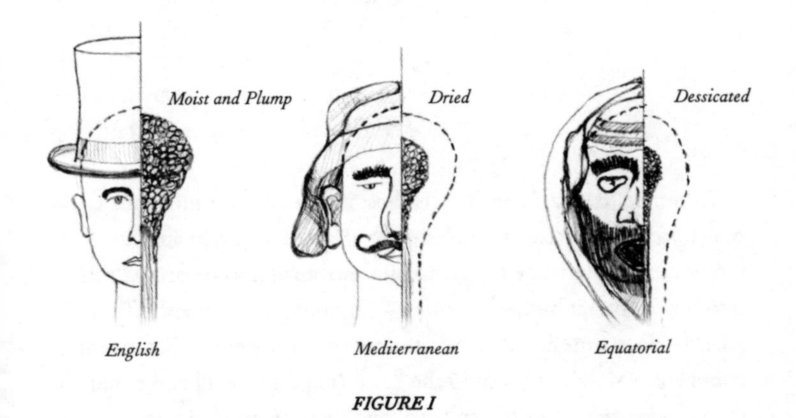

FIGURE I

I need scarcely mention that in the southern hemisphere the position is reversed. Thus, for instance, the prevailing idiocy in Borneo or Sumatra gives way to greater rationality as one descends southwards towards the cooler parts of the Antipodes, just as the aggression and intermittent bestiality of the Australians yields to the gentility of the New Zealanders.

As an additional point, it is worth noting that the supremacy of the British nation is no mere accident, for we live at the lines of latitude most favourable to balanced brain activity – a fact which explains why our Teutonic cousins at similar latitudes have occasionally rivalled us in the philosophical, mechanical and scientific spheres. For just as intelligence falls below a certain latitude, *so does it fall above it!*

FIGURE 2

In simple, layman's terms it is thus. At the equator the brain's moisture is mostly steam. At latitude 51° 28' N – that of the Greenwich Observatory – the brain's moisture has condensed fully into liquid. But at higher latitudes – beginning to the north of Aberdeen, at latitude 57° 9' N – the colder climes mean that ice commences slowly to form in the brain (see Fig. 2). This accounts for the recalcitrance of northern Scots and the slow pace of life throughout Scandinavia. Once inside the Arctic Circle a goodly proportion of the brain is iced, and therefore sluggish and slow-moving – a fact which explains every aspect of Esquimaux existence.

I trust the foregoing explains the matter simply and conclusively.

Yours &c.
J. Selman-Troytt

JOURNAL NOTES FOR JANUARY 19TH, 1913

Curious meeting with Newton today. He came in to discuss his problem with involuntary emission, just as he has done every day for the past twenty-seven months, but then suddenly he burst out with the extraordinary news that he does not suffer from involuntary emission at all, and never has done! In a fit of candour he revealed that he had fabricated the problem to conceal his embarrassment over the real reason for his visits, which was to reveal that he received sinful gratification from wearing his wife's mother's clothing. However, and this is the very noteworthy part, his gratification is *not* obtained in the same way as that of Col. Morrison, who dresses in Mrs Morrison's gowns in order to pirouette in front of his servants, but from wearing only his mother-in-law's undergarments – the various petticoats, bloomers, hooped underskirts and so on of the type she has favoured since the 1860s. He revealed that he was actually wearing them under his own clothing at that very moment, and explained that it was their presence inside his waistcoat and trousers that accounted for the tremendous bloating of his lower torso and legs. I had wondered, because he seemed some eight stones* heavier than when I removed his wart during dinner at Castellini's just last week.

I did my best to explain to him that the compulsion to dress in his mother-in-law's clothing resulted from a brain abnormality, and that there was little that could be done because an operation on the brain, even assuming the exact site of the deviancy could be isolated, would likely prove fatal. I recommended a generic trepanning, but explained that I was not sanguine about its efficacy. He left disconsolate, taking very small steps with his ankles forced a good yard apart because of the displacement in his thighs.

* 51kg

Journal notes for February 9th, 1913

I feel I must make haste with the lotion research. If Aunt dies before it is finished, the whole project will be rendered redundant and my notes worthless.

Journal notes for March 3rd, 1913

Significant staining. I did not wish to draw Fairbanks' attention to it, but was unsuccessful in removing it myself with lye.

Journal notes for March 27th, 1913

Dalwood next door complains again at the noise of hammering as we attempt a minor modification on the cantilever arm. Again! He says it is the fifth day in a row. Oaf! As though existing measures for sound muffling were insufficient. I hate Dalwood! I have no time for a man with neither wit nor grace. He is a tedious, impudent dullard! I think I have always loathed him, with his pitted skin and shiny, ridiculous pate. And so jumped-up and pompous... As if he could ever speak of anything of the slightest interest to anyone but another dullard! I refused to receive him and sent Fairbanks to remonstrate with him on the steps. Perhaps I should have had him tipped down them!

JOURNAL NOTES FOR APRIL 4TH, 1913

Soup strange again, with a kind of metallic aftertaste reminiscent of sucking a thruppenny bit*. I have consulted the kitchen records and find this to be the second occasion upon which this has happened in nine years. Not conclusive, but may be grounds for further observation.

Something, possibly a hyacinth, bloomed in the garden overnight.

JOURNAL NOTES FOR APRIL 18TH, 1913

Extraordinary interview today with Sir Robert Kingsland and wife, both of whom state emphatically that the marriage has never been consummated despite the woman having given birth to four children in the past five years. When I raised this point she denied that the children were hers. She brought one of the children with her as 'evidence'. But as evidence of what?Whilst they sat before me, the woman twice gave violent jerking downward eye and head movements that were clear invitations to examine her private areas. It was as though she longed for them to be exposed. Throughout, her husband simply smiled vacantly as though afflicted by idiocy. Very unsettling. I was glad when they left.

---

* A three-penny piece (3*d*) in pre-decimal British coinage. The twelve-sided coin was often sucked in place of a mint at informal functions.

Journal notes for April 21st, 1913

When I sat to my writing today I found that my hand trembled slightly. I have no explanation.

Journal notes for April 22nd, 1913

Trembling again.

Journal notes for April 23rd, 1913

Trembling again.

Journal notes for April 24th, 1913

Trembling gone! A mystery.

Romance

Maud Cleeg

Only daughter of Silas and Veronica Cleeg, the Malvern socialites, Maud was indulged as a child and given the freedom of the family's Dunbartonshire estate whilst her parents were absent for months at a time attending a succession of events on the Malvern social calendar. Bored and recalcitrant, she once dismissed and re-hired the entire estate staff eleven times in a single weekend, simply for the pleasure of watching them pack and unpack their luggage.

Maud had little patience with social conventions and was not above laughing suddenly and out of context at the sound of unexpected flatulence, even if it were not her own.

As an adult she was frequently loud and abrasive, but acquaintances knew that this masked an inner sadness, for the words '*My life is a confusing sea of misery in which I feel myself drowning. I am surrounded by despair. Blackness. All is blackness.*' recur often in her letters.

Her affair with Jeremy was covered extensively in the press but never consummated. There is little doubt that Selman-Troytt was in love with her. On one occasion, when she was particularly melancholy, he paid an organ grinder in Hyde Park to pass wind so that her spirits could be lifted.

J. SELMAN-TROYTT, ESQ.,
14 BERKELEY SQUARE, LONDON, W.

Sir Charles Callwell,
Director of Military Operations,
War Office,
Whitehall,
London, W.

18 November, 1914

Dear Sir,

Following the dreadful news from Ypres, I am entreated by my brother Jonty to make representation to you in the hope that you will allow him to assist our country in her time of greatest need.

Heavy casualties and battle losses have increased the number of men who will not be returning to these shores, and my brother's thoughts have been often with the sweethearts and widows of these brave souls. He is concerned not only for their emotional and physical welfare, as they struggle with the loneliness and isolation of having no bed-mate, but also for the welfare of the nation now that future generations of new potential soldiers, who should have been born but could not be born because intercourse that should have taken place could not take place because the male partner was deceased, will not now be born. My brother seeks to redress this.

As you may be aware, my brother's seed is very strong (according to our family records he has never performed intercourse without impregnating the recipient), and he now offers this seed in the service of His Majesty's government. In order to assist with the rapid repopulation of the British Isles he is willing to impregnate any woman put before him. He calculates that he is capable of 9 insertions per day, allowing for 65 minutes between insertions to recharge his testicles with seminal fluid. He suggests that the 65-minute intervals might be used by someone – perhaps a clergyman or a nun – to calm the women and make them ready for his ministrations.

As to the logistics, patently it will be less efficient if my brother requires to travel to the homes of these women, particularly if they were to live, say, in Cornwall, Kent and Dunbartonshire, and he were expected to commute between them in the course of a single day. His own suggestion is that a hospital ward be requisitioned and prepared, as it can be pressed into service both as an arena of conception, and as a place of delivery many months later for those who have carried their child to term.

At the rate of 63 impregnations per week (or 3,150 per annum, allowing for the two weeks he would still wish to spend grouse shooting), Jonty calculates that he can father over 7,000 children before the war comes to a conclusion, taking account of the incidence of multiple births that will be occasioned by the strength of his seed.

As an act of charity in time of war my brother makes no demands for his services, save that the women should be between the ages of 18 and 45 in order to increase the chances of his seed taking root. He makes no discrimination on the grounds of wealth, appearance, weight or heritage, for it is his contention that all women are deserving of impregnation. He feels that all have suffered equal loss, and that all should be treated equally in receiving a gift that can bring comfort to their hearts and satisfaction to their loins. His one request is that any women who are staunch Methodists should have their faces covered with some kind of mask.

He begs leave to advise you that he can be at your disposal within 65 minutes of receiving your summons.

Awaiting your advises I remain

Your most humble and obedient servant in these darkened hours,

J. Selman-Troytt

Family

Jonty and offspring

A small selection of the ninety-seven children (above) fathered by Jeremy's brother, Jonty (right).

Birth records show that the Selman-Troytts were unusually fecund, but Jonty seems to have been particularly fertile even by the standards of this family. He produced a constant stream of children between 1871 and 1939 when, at the age of 83, he inexplicably became impotent.

Jonty's voracious sexual appetite was legendary. On one occasion he had to be forcibly restrained from having intercourse with his wife only seconds after the delivery of their 23rd child.* The attending physician, who was in the process of cutting the umbilicus when Jonty jostled him aside '*in a state of extreme engorgement*', was compelled to lay the newborn down in order to wrestle her father to the floor with the assistance of the midwife and four servants. The doctor was amazed to record that Jonty's '*engorgement did not subside, even under continual intravenous sedation, although we maintained constant observation of it throughout a period of 67 hours.*'

Jonty eschewed the use of any form of contraception, maintaining emphatically that '*women were designed to be filled – anyone can see that!*' After copulation, he insisted that all partners should lie prone for a period of twelve hours to '*increase the chance of my seed laying down roots*'.

Jonty's greatest ambition was to impregnate the birth control campaigner Marie Stopes, to whom he always referred as '*a perfect vessel in need of filling.*' Although he was never successful, she was so impressed by his persistence that she awarded Jonty a congratulatory medal to mark every hundredth repetition of his invitation to '*gouge [her] verdant valley with [his] rough, pointed glacier.*'

---

* Joyce

Social & Sexual Etiquette

BY

JEREMY SELMAN-TROYTT

O'Rourke & LeFevre
London
MCMXVI

Introduction

THE FIRST MEETING WITH A prospective marital partner can be a frightening experience. The man may not know what to say or what parts may be touched, and at what stage. The woman may stand mute, ignorant as to what type of contact may be appropriate or whether the man's features are correct. The result, in both parties, is fear.

The simple rules that follow lay down established protocols that will lessen the chance of errors, increase confidence and minimise the possibility of ridicule, shame and humiliation.

PART ONE: Preparations for the Romantic Introduction

THE COUPLE SHOULD ALWAYS BE introduced by an independent third party, whose impartiality is beyond question and who cannot later be accused of lobbying for congress on behalf of either the first or second party. The third party should remain within earshot, in order to provide a sense of security and to escort either the first or second party from the scene once the meeting is concluded.

The meeting place may be a crowded train station, a secluded woodland glade, a field, a park, a museum, a restaurant, another's house, or even a more intimate setting.[1] The choice of venue is important, since it can have a significant effect upon the success of the encounter. It is for this reason that many opt for romantic venues that will provide a sympathetic environment for their importunings. The Scottish Highlands have been found particularly effective in this regard, but Kew Gardens, the Lake District and Boulogne are also favoured locales.

[Some omitted here. Ed.*]*

Heavyweight clothing is not essential except in the Scottish Highlands, but all parties will benefit from a quality serge twill to protect elbows and knees from abrasion in rocky terrain. Where gorse is prevalent, gaiters should be worn.

Punctuality is paramount, so it will be necessary to set out early in the morning if the rendezvous is far distant. However, the wise participant will travel up the day before in order to settle in and leave time for a restful sleep before the meeting.

Immediately prior to the meeting, those of a nervous disposition may derive benefit from a few moments spent in quite contemplation within a church or other place of sanctuary. A full and frank discussion with a minister concerning physical matters may also be soothing at this point.

It is recommended that the first meeting should last longer than one minute but no longer than fifteen minutes. In the normal course of events, one party would expect to speak during only half of the encounter, with the other taking responsibility for the remainder, but the careful planner will leave nothing to chance and

[1] Although if any initial physical exploration is to be proposed by either the Lady or the Gentleman then heed must be taken of the notes and precautions in Appendix MCV.

it is best to assume that the other party will say nothing at all. Therefore one should prepare and rehearse conversation to fill fifteen minutes. This quantity can be calculated according to Weissbein's figures on mean speech speeds in Norfolk in 1876, as reproduced in the following table:

Rate of Speech	*Mean Average Words Spoken In Every Minute*
Extraordinarily Slow	25 MAWSIEM
Very Slow	40 MAWSIEM
Quite Slow	80 MAWSIEM
Slow	120 MAWSIEM
Medium	200 MAWSIEM
Fast	300 MAWSIEM
Very Fast	500 MAWSIEM
Hyper-Kinetic	850 MAWSIEM
Unintelligible	1200 MAWSIEM

Using the formula T = W x M[1], it can be seen that for a person with a 'Medium' speech speed some 3,000 words (200 x 15) should be prepared for a fifteen-minute meeting, whereas someone who is 'Unintelligible' should prepare 18,000. For those made anxious by conversing extemporaneously, everything should be written out beforehand and committed to memory.

[*Seven pages omitted here.* Ed.]

It is not necessary for either party to have an enema before the meeting because ordinary levels of flatulence can be controlled with regular doses of common liver salts. However, if the flatulence is excessive due to nervous dyspepsia, or if either party will obtain

[1] T = Total; W = Words; M = Minutes

emotional or spiritual relief from the procedure, then an enema may be carried out. However, it should be administered only by a physician, a servant or a close friend. Do *not* be tempted, as a means of creating greater intimacy, to wait until the actual meeting in order to ask your prospective spouse to administer it. The danger here is that the obverse could occur. Indeed, many Gentlemen are made uncomfortable by the procedure for administering an enema to a Lady and would prefer to endure her flatulence. In any event, intimacy cannot be hurried by such fabricated catalysts and must proceed at its own natural pace.

PART TWO: The Romantic Introduction

AT FIRST MEETING, A GENTLEMAN should always present a gift to the Lady. This should not be money or food. It should be a token of his love and respect, as well as a sign of his undying devotion in the event that the meeting should lead to a permanent union. Birds are an excellent choice as gifts, as very few Ladies remain unmoved in the presence of a living thing. However other animals may also be presented, provided that safety and practicality are borne in mind during the selection procedure. There is no need to conduct extensive analysis in order to determine whether potential gifts are safe and practical. Common sense ought to suffice. For example, birds, cats and caged Lepidoptera would be appropriate; reptiles or stoats would be unsafe; fish, bison or an ocelot would be impractical.

The Lady should accept the gift, whatever it is, graciously and with an appropriate display of gratitude and affection. She should convey that it holds deep meaning for her, even if she intends to dispose of it summarily at the conclusion of the meeting. If her hands become soiled while receiving the gift then she should wipe them discreetly and never with an ostentatious display of displeasure lest the Gentleman become disheartened and lose interest in prosecuting the encounter.

[Two pages omitted here. Ed.*]*

The parties may now introduce their proposed topics for conversation, whether pre-rehearsed or *extempore.* However if neither is comfortable with speech then it is quite permissible to sit or stand in silence for long periods, and the more far-sighted will prepare for this eventually by bringing with them some means of diversion. This may be a book or puzzle or, in the case of the Lady, some needlepoint.

In the event that the parties elect to embark upon conversation, there are many topics that can prove fertile starting points: fashion (Lady), sporting wagers or feats of daring (Gentleman), weather (both), grouse shooting (Gentleman), needlepoint (Lady), dog fighting (Gentleman), exfoliation (both), heroes of romantic fiction (Lady), fox hunting (both), noted débutantes of the Season (Lady), avian welfare (both).

Certain topics must be approached with caution, or avoided altogether, as they may provoke embarrassment owing to the Lady's inability to participate with sufficient confidence and aplomb. Political matters, science, commerce, philosophy, economics and current affairs are prominent among these.

Both parties should aim for a certain naturalness in their discourse so that conversation does not appear forced. Strained discourse may have a deleterious effect upon the confidence of one's interlocutor and can significantly reduce the chances of later congress. Consider the following examples, and compare the strained speech of the first with the naturalness of the second:

Example 1

G: I am most honoured to make your gracious acquaintance, and I trust that you will not consider me rude or presumptuous if I render you a compliment by stipulating that the Highland air, while bracing, is not so much a tonic for the system, nor so much a stimulation for the senses, as the sight of your exquisite features.

L: Thank you.

G: Upon occasions such as these, when one shuns rational thought and surrenders one's senses to the erratic guidance of irrational feeling, it is intoxication of the mind by a surfeit of aesthetic impulses which causes one to stumble in giddy joyfulness in the presence of such a superabundance of visual stimulus.

L: Thank you.

G: I fear you may think me loquacious but exhort you to believe that my tongue does no more than give felicitous utterance to the effervescence that arises within me at the sight of your beauteous form, and I beg you to comprehend that such uncharacteristic verbosity is urged upon me by the concomitant anticipation I experience at the prospect that we may become joined in spiritual and physical union during the procreational process.

L: Thank you.

. . . &c.

Example 2

G: I am euphoric that you have elected to rendezvous here in the shadows of such inspiring peaks, although the awe which they strike within me is dwarfed by the exultation which your beauty arouses.

L: Thank you.

G: I offer you this parrot as a token of my love, my devotion and my lifelong gratitude that you have consented to this meeting knowing that it might one day necessitate congress. I am flattered that you consider me not too repellent, and ask you to accept this bird as an expression of the admiration and respect I feel for the compassion, warmth, charity and understanding you have displayed already by setting aside your natural sense of repugnance during the contemplation and acceptance of an act of such violation that it cannot fail to leave you overcome with shame, remorse and humiliation.

L: Thank you.

G: I entreat you to take the greatest care with its handling, for its beak and claws are sharp and its continence unpredictable. However, these minor disadvantages notwithstanding, it is my fervent hope that the bird can be encouraged into the mimicry of your voice so that its repetitions may remain as a record of the mellifluous nature of your paralinguistic communication for as long as it lives.

L: Thank you.

. . . &c.

Physical contact at first meeting may be acceptable if a prior request is made and acceded to in writing as part of the preparations for introduction. In fact, provided the request is formulated according to the protocols specified in Appendix XXII (p.mvccxxii), then many forms of physical contact are permissible upon first meeting. These include exploratory palpation, an examination of the teeth or checking for the presence of a hair-piece.

Closer intimacy, however, is not typical at first meeting unless both parties are Methodists, and it is more common simply to hold hands or explore the face with fingertips. Neither activity should be attempted without first cleansing the hands if they have been in recent contact with uncooked shellfish. For this eventuality, it is permissible for either party to carry with them a small quantity of salt with which to prepare a 'brine rinse' to remove unpleasant odours.

[Ninety-two pages omitted here. Ed.*]*

PART FOUR: Becoming Engaged

IF THE LADY IS OFFENSIVE in appearance then it will be necessary for a significant dowry to be negotiated in order to overcome doubts that may be held by the Gentleman. The size of the dowry is always in inverse proportion to the attractiveness of the Lady. The negotiations will take place between the Lady's father and either the Gentleman or the Gentleman's financial representative.

The process generally follows a strict protocol, and after an initial handshake it is customary for the Lady's father to begin the proceedings with the phrase 'I open the bidding at . . .', before suggesting a figure he believes to be commensurate with the offensiveness of his daughter. It will then be for the other party to accept or reject the father's opening bid or any subsequent proposals.

However, if the Lady is attractive, or the Gentleman is offensive, then the process may be reversed, with the Gentleman or the Gentleman's financial representative beginning negotiations with 'I open the bidding at . . .'

If the Lady is very attractive, and is highly sought after because she shows promise as a companion as well as a vessel for procreation, then it is possible that other suitors may be in attendance and that an auction with aggressive bidding will evolve. In this event, the Gentleman should use his own judgement to set a *maximum* value upon the Lady, and should determine in advance that he will not exceed this bid. A friend should remain on hand to ensure that he remains within his predetermined limits.

Once an appropriate sum is bid and accepted then the contract for engagement is deemed 'binding'. A handshake seals the bargain and a date for wedding and coupling is set. Barring the premature death of either party, marriage, congress and procreation will now take their natural course.

The Gentleman now buys a ring for his 'fiancée' in order to claim possession and to signify that the ordeal of congress is one that both will soon face.

[Eighteen pages omitted here. Ed.*]*

PART FIVE: The Wedding Night

IF THE PARTIES HAVE INDULGED to excess in food or drink at any antecedent function then they may choose to rest before congress to lessen the chance that what they are about to undergo may cause them to regurgitate.

[One page omitted here. Ed.*]*

Congress will require that the parts of both parties be uncovered. The parties may choose to disrobe completely but in any event they will require to expose their parts at the minimum.

Neither party should undress the other. Any lack of familiarity with the habiliments of the other gender will cause a *faux pas* and may increase embarrassment beyond endurable limits. For those unused to undressing themselves, it is permissible to have a servant on hand to perform one's disinvestment.

At this stage there may be some confusion about the parts, with neither party being able to identify his or her own part, or the part of the other party. In this case, reference should be made to the diagrams on pages mmlvii and mmcclxxviii in Appendices LXI and CCXIX at the end of this volume. It will be more efficient if each party has his or her own separate copy of the diagrams during the identification procedure. Each part should be named aloud and committed to memory as each is identified, in order to dispense with the impediment of holding a book in one's hand throughout the remainder of the procedure.

[Four pages omitted here. Ed.*]*

Those Gentlemen unwilling or unable to retract their own prepuces may have a servant do this for them. An alternative would be the use of a prepuce retractor. There are no proprietary models available at present (although that situation may change at any moment) so a pair of coal tongs may be pressed into service. It goes without saying that these should be sterilised first by boiling for twenty minutes and then plunging them into iodine.

According to convention, tumescence will have commenced at the unveiling of the Lady's part. During the next stage the Lady should move forward two steps and hold the Gentleman's prepuce to encourage this tumescence (see Figure xviii, Appendix XLV). If tumescence has *not* commenced, refer to Appendix MMIV for advice and suggestions.

If the Gentleman is a sodomite who has married for the sake of form, position or money, and if he cannot obtain sufficient arousal or stimulation from the sight of the Lady's part for him to fulfil his conjugal responsibilities, then it is permissible for a male friend to be brought into the room so that he can engage the Gentleman in provocative conversation of a type liable to stimulate arousal of his part so that the union can proceed.

[Three pages omitted here. Ed.*]*

I am often asked: 'What is congress?' This question is addressed in detail in Appendix LVIII, together with diagrams and an illustration of two newts. However, in simple scientific terms congress requires that *the part of the party of the first part part the part of the party of the second part.*

[Forty-two pages omitted here. Ed.*]*

The Gentleman, no matter how great his misgivings about the prospect of the union, and no matter how desirous of a swift conclusion he may be, should resist the temptation to run at the Lady and effect ephemeral penetration at speed. Although such a strategy may appear efficacious with regard to breaching the hymen, the opportunity for error and subsequent injury is high.

Instead, the Lady should lay supine with her part uncovered (see Figure xxii – Newt 'A' – Appendix LIX). The Gentleman, having apologised in advance for what is about to happen, should give a discreet cough to signal his approach and afford the Lady time to avert her face. He should then lower himself slowly into the position illustrated in Figure xxiii (Newt 'B').

[Eleven pages omitted here. Ed.*]*

If the Lady believes palpation to be in order then the Gentleman should not demur or withdraw from her touch. He should lie quiescent during pronation or supination.

Although it is common practice to utilise an extender at this point, a similar result may be achieved with any implement that is long enough to bridge the gap and to which a small piece of wire can be affixed with twine. The Lady may then laugh if she feels inclined; indeed, she should be encouraged to do so if it is agreed by all parties that to do so may help her to relax. Her back should be arched slightly and her right leg bent at the knee and crossed below the left in a 'figure 4' formation (see Figure iv, Appendix LXI). The gentleman's head should be held away, and slightly to the right, so the lady is not discommoded by his breathing. He may produce a sound of slight strain at the conclusion.

If notification has been requested by parents, a telegram may be sent at this juncture.

[Four pages omitted here. Ed.*]*

It remains only to conclude this section with a reference to weight. Congress with an obese partner presents a series of physical, aesthetic and olfactory challenges, since not only will the participants be repulsed by the sight of surplus flesh but physical hurdles will certainly intervene. For example, a thin Gentleman may not be able to reach the parts of an obese Lady, and a thin Lady may be incapable of bearing the weight of an obese Gentleman. Under such conditions it is advisable, even essential, to enlist the help of household staff. In the case of an obese Lady, for example, the assistance of two servants to hold fast her legs whilst the Gentleman attempts to locate her part will render the experience faster and less distressing for all. Similarly, two servants can be given the task of supporting an obese Gentleman and lowering him gently onto a smaller partner so that she is not crushed or asphyxiated. A third servant can be on hand to wipe the perspiration from his back.

Congress between two obese people creates many logistical

problems and is beyond the scope of this section of the guide. However, the challenge of procreation with an obese partner is discussed in more depth in the part entitled: 'Procreation and the Effect of Weight'.

[Four hundred and seventy pages omitted here. Ed.*]*

PART NINE: Miscellaneous Considerations

No gentleman must allow his prepuce to become offensive.

[Some omitted here. Ed.*]*

A glans must be sanitised before presentation. No Lady will be attracted to an unsanitised glans. The glans may be sanitised by swabbing with alcohol or acetone. In the absence of these, it may be immersed briefly in boiling water. A Gentleman should *never* ask a Lady to sanitise his glans.

[Some omitted here. Ed.*]*

If there is evidence of exfoliation then neither party should view it with repugnance. Small-scale scaling is to be expected where open skin contact causes the tissue to dehydrate and friction loosens the dead cells. It is permissible for either party to halt proceedings and request the application of an emollient.

[Remainder omitted. Ed.*]*

Patients

The Withenshaw Rhinoplasty

The Withenshaw case became public in the summer of 1916.

Ernest Withenshaw, a wealthy American with a very large nose, had arrived in London for surgical consultations about having it reduced. Although the procedure was potentially fatal, he was determined to go ahead, for his nose was of such a size that he had difficulty seeing past it. Withenshaw could maintain binocularity of vision only by turning his whole head in the direction he wanted to look, and friends often said that from the side he resembled a chameleon.

What happened during Withenshaw's sojourn in London is the subject of conflicting versions. According to Mr. Beaconsfield, consultant surgeon, Withenshaw arrived for discussion of his nose, took tea, asked several questions, and then left to consider the matter further.

According to Withenshaw he arrived at Beaconsfield's consulting rooms at 4 o'clock, and was in the middle of eating a cucumber sandwich when he was 'attacked from behind and felt an enormous cloth pressed over [his] nose and mouth'. He remembered nothing more until he resurfaced through a fog of anaesthetic to find himself gazing up at a ring of intent male faces. He felt something being done to his face, and then lapsed back into unconsciousness. Then, awaking in his hotel room, he discovered that his septum had been removed along with both nostrils, and that the upper cartilage had been joined directly to the philtrum, so that his nose now formed a solid bridge between his eyebrows and his upper lip. His personal doctor suggested that Withenshaw may have been the subject of a bizarre experiment.

The police were called and Withenshaw identified one of the men as Beaconsfield, and another as Jeremy Selman-Troytt.

Selman-Troytt denied any knowledge of the affair, saying that he was occupied with testing a prepuce retractor on a servant at the time in question. A few days later the case collapsed when Withenshaw unexpectedly left the country following a quiet dinner with John and Jonas Selman-Troytt*, his hotel room left empty except for a note which stated that he had had a change of heart, was completely happy with his new appearance, and had decided to celebrate with an extended tour of South America that might last several years.

The police announced themselves satisfied and Selman-Troytt was able to return to his lotions.

* See p.85.

Journal notes for August 3rd, 1916

Nothing from Stanleyson today.

J. SELMAN-TROYTT, ESQ.,
14 BERKELEY SQUARE, LONDON, W.

Moss & Co,
Bicycle Repairers & Engineers,
12 Railway Cuttings,
Eastcheap

1 September, 1916

Moss,

Your boy has just returned my tricycle in exactly the same condition as when I submitted it to you for repair! Are you incompetent, or simply insolent? My previous letter to you stated quite clearly that I wished for the frame to be repainted, the saddle re-covered, and the tyres re-shod. When I visited your workshop yesterday you assured me that you understood those instructions. You heard me say them clearly three times, and even asked me what colour of paint should be used on the frame. Yet none of this work has been carried out! I have examined the machine closely and there is no evidence that you have so much as touched it. Notwithstanding this, not only do you return it now for my 'approval' but you have the audacity to enclose a bill for 10 guineas 'To recondition one small tricycle'. Either you are an idiot, or you are a mendacious fraud. I am incandescent with rage at your effrontery. Perhaps you think me a fool? I assure you I am not. If the work on my tricycle is not carried out properly by tomorrow afternoon then I will not be held responsible for my actions, nor for those of any unknown persons who may choose to enter into your house and cause you and your family actual bodily harm with a blunt instrument of some unspecified type.

J. Selman-Troytt

Patients

'Celia Calhoun'

Able-Seaman Plackett in 1916, photographed just hours after the transformation into 'Celia Calhoun' which allowed him to join the W.R.N.S.

When news of the forthcoming formation of the Women's Royal Naval Service (or 'Wrens' as it was popularly known) was announced in 1915, Plackett became one of dozens of professional sailors determined to switch to a branch of the service they felt was more suited to their disposition, sensitivities, needs and inclinations. Plackett spoke for many naval men when he stated: 'I had always loved the Royal Navy, even from when I was a child . . . but somehow I never felt properly at home in the men's branch. There just weren't enough opportunities for a good old natter if there were things you wanted to get off your chest. And the uniform could be unflattering too, especially if you didn't have the hips for it.'

Contrary to rumours circulating at the time, Selman-Troytt did not perform surgery on Plackett. Instead he gave Plackett an hour's intensive counselling to prepare him emotionally for life as a fully-fledged woman. He then advised him on certain cosmetic changes necessary to make him look more feminine (this was a significant challenge as Plackett had boxed for the navy). Finally, he designed and fashioned a labial prosthesis from ivory which, when fitted, concealed 'Celia's' gender completely even when 'she' was wearing something as close-fitting as a swimming costume.

The prosthesis was shaped somewhat like a pony saddle, and was fastened into Plackett's groin with his genitals concealed above and behind it. It worked by separating his testicles on either side of its upper ridge, and then compressing each of them between his thigh and the side plate of the prosthesis when the groin-fixing buckles were tightened firmly. His penile shaft rested in a special hollow on the top of the 'saddle', where it resided in complete comfort as long as it remained detumescent.

According to Plackett, the prosthesis was 'very comfortable provided [he] did not walk or swell'. In the event that he was in stimulating company and began to tumesce then it could become painful enough to cause him to double up. He found walking particularly difficult because moving his legs without discomfort was impossible with each testicle highly compressed against his thigh.

However, when the Wrens opened their doors to new recruits, 'Celia Calhoun' was standing proudly in line and was among the first to sign up.

'Celia' was accepted and posted to HMS Invincible. The ship's duty log records that 'Calhoun performs her duties quite satisfactorily but rather slowly. She would be a more useful recruit if she placed her legs closer together when she walks. There are some corridors too narrow for her to enter . . .'

The imposture was discovered after only four months at sea, when Plackett was surprised in a toilet cubicle with his skirt and prosthesis held aloft as he relieved himself. The incident was widely covered in the national press, Selman-Troytt finding himself praised and vilified in equal measure. However, he proved typically indifferent to external comment and wrote to *The Times*: 'Scientific exploration has always required the courage to break boundaries and pursue conclusions without fear of the consequences. As a dispassionate man of science I am immune to criticism as a matter of necessity.'

Again he was the recipient of several death threats, some of which seemed in greater earnest than their predecessors. However, Selman-Troytt dismissed them all, especially the one that purported to be from his own brothers, Jonah, John and Jonas. He had Fairbanks consign the letters to the fire while he returned to studying blueprints for some proposed modifications to the retractor.

CONTROVERSIAL SCIENTIST FOUND DEAD

Jeremy Selman-Troytt (48), son of glazing magnate Josiah Selman-Troytt (96), and an heir to the Selman-Troytt Empire, was yesterday tragically killed when he was crushed beneath falling masonry.

Mr. Selman-Troytt was taking his usual post-prandial tri-cycling excursion around Berkeley Square, down Berkeley Street and along Piccadilly when he had the grave misfortune to be struck by several large blocks that somehow detached themselves from the Kennett building on the corner of Half Moon Street.

Witnesses strolling nearby were shocked by the incident. Mr. J Solomon (66), a retired felt-brusher from Knightsbridge, informed this correspondent: 'One minute he was tri-cycling very quickly towards me, his body bent forward and his legs a blur as he thrust the pedals around, and the next thing I knew he lay unmoving beneath an enormous pile of masonry. It was not something you see every day.'

From The Times, *6 November 1916*

Appendectomies

Appendix I

From the Foreword to Finding Selman-Troytt
by Finlay Finlayson *(see p.248)**, published in 1951*

A fitting place to begin one's examination of the life of any man is in summarising one's first encounter with him. In that way we may chart how one's initial curiosity about another man, having begun as a mere quickening of interest, may lead to a compulsion, and finally to an obsession that eclipses all else. So I like to think it was with my relationship with Selman-Troytt.

Ridiculous as it may now seem to relate, I had not even heard of Jeremy Selman-Troytt by the time the recent war broke out! A quick résumé of my circumstances at that time will serve to put my ignorance into context.

In the autumn of 1938 I went up to Oxford to read Politics and Philosophy. After graduation I hoped to write a doctoral thesis on Redundant Hypotheses as part of an academic career decided upon in consultation with my father who, seeing that I had little practical or commercial bent, was determined to guide me into a field of endeavour that he considered a match for my talents, such as he saw them.

However the war was soon to intervene and place these aspirations in jeopardy. The first rumblings reached the ears of my father in early 1939, and he advised me quickly to take a sabbatical from my studies and join the armed forces while there were still plenty of vacancies in the better positions. He guided me into the RAF, where I began my flight training as a newly commissioned Pilot Officer in the summer of 1939, just a few weeks before my nineteenth birthday.

I found flying to be enormously challenging, in part because I lack manual dexterity and coordination, but most particularly because of recurring problems with motion sickness. I had always had a delicate constitution, not able even to countenance the slight rolling of a punt on the Cherwell, so an aeroplane ride, particularly if there was turbulence, caused me considerable distress and discomfort.

Older hands advised me that the condition would pass within a matter of weeks, as my brain and stomach conditioned themselves, but it did not. The slightest departure from level flight could cause me to regurgitate violently, often without warning, and to the profound frustration of my instructors. As time passed, I became disconsolate and feared for my future. I became yet more despondent when word reached me, via the chaplain, that my uniform had become a cause for concern among my superiors. Indeed, so soiled did my garments become that I was twice compelled to press my father for completely new uniforms because the old ones were beyond the scope even of a vigorous sponging, the material having become so impregnated and stiffened that it had become difficult to bend either knees or elbows. In that respect it was not unlike wearing armour. As the discarded uniforms were of no further use to me I decided to donate them to the war effort, giving them to a local charity providing clothing for disadvantaged children.

Fortunately, my nausea was not a sufficient impediment to prevent me from serving my country, and when I was finally declared fit for active service I was transferred to France, where I began flying solo surveillance missions in the autumn of 1939, just two days before war was officially declared by Mr. Chamberlain.

However, I had the very great misfortune to be captured early on in the conflict and was forced to spend the rest of the war incarcerated behind enemy lines. This was a traumatic experience for a young man of only nineteen, cut off, bewildered and abused by people who often punched me without warning and shouted at me in guttural voices that made no sense to my untrained ear. Many years later, by the end of my captivity, I had become proficient enough in the German language to do many everyday things, such as ordering lentils or a shoehorn, or returning a bag of inferior toffee; but in those early days I recall it as no more than a shudder-inducing cacophony that thundered around me and conspired to steal away the last fragment of my hope and undermine my sanity. I feel no shame now in acknowledging the fact that I was very frightened, although I resolved, as all Englishmen did in that dark period, to await my fate with whatever stoicism I could muster. What a change it all seemed from the tranquillity of my parents' home in Bayswater, where the silence was so complete that the ticking of a grandfather clock could be heard clearly resounding through all five floors!

Fortunately, in the earliest days of my imprisonment, not all of my captors were unkind or brutal. Although German, some were the sons of gentlemen, and would never dream of stooping to the physical abuse of another human being. I remember one, Herr Glissold, boasting proudly that he had never once assaulted a prisoner during interrogation. Of course, the war was then only three days old so it is always possible that he did not sustain this level of humanitarianism throughout the rest of the conflict. He treated me very kindly, however, allowing me unrestricted use of the bathing facilities in the west wing of Schloss Streinevold, the Glissold family seat. But this period of calm was not to endure. Several days later, the luxurious accommodation at Schloss Streinevold a fading memory, I found myself en route to incarceration proper at *Prolag 1* (*Vilsbiburg*).

Many readers will be very familiar with the German detention camps known as *Stalags* (derived from the German noun ***Stammlager***, meaning 'permanent camps') a term made much more famous recently by wonderful films such as *The Wooden Horse**, which some of you may

* Very popular British World War II film directed by Jack Lee, and released in 1950. It is based on the true story of a group of British prisoners of war who built a wooden horse and used it in an attempt to gain covert entry to Berchtesgaten with the aim of assassinating Hitler. In Lee's version the horse is a very large and elaborate model made from matches horded painstakingly over years, and in an ironic twist the plan fails when

have seen at the pictures. However, many fewer readers will be familiar with the *Prolags* (***Pro**visorium**lag**er* or 'provisional camps') that preceded them, and which were intended as temporary staging posts and modest places of detention prior to the construction of the much larger, more permanent, and more expensive Stalags.

The difference was considerable. *Stalag VIIA*, for example, constructed later in the war in not so distant Moosburg, was built over the course of ten months, at significant cost in money and slave labour, on about eighty-five acres of land, to house up to ten thousand prisoners of war. *Prolag 1 (Vilsbiburg)*, in stark contrast, was built on a very small plot next to an unused grape silo, using local materials of the flimsiest kind, over the course of six days by a small team of Carpathian farm labourers abducted while they were building a dry-stone wall near Bratislava, and was intended as the temporary home for anything up to thirty-two 'transient' prisoners before their onward transhipment to more permanent camps.

In the event, evolving circumstances caused the German High Command to make certain deviations from this plan – deviations that were to impact upon captors as well as captives – and some *Prolags* stayed in service far longer than had been envisaged originally by the military strategists.

I arrived eventually at *Prolag 1 (Vilsbiburg)* after an exhausting journey which began near dawn with me being driven very slowly and considerately to Stuttgart railway station by Herr Glissold's chauffeur, a fastidious man who glanced nervously at the upholstery whenever I shifted position. During the drive I was very glad of the warmth of my fur-lined flying jacket and boots, as the majestic Mercedes was open in the *tonneau* and the early September air exceedingly brisk. I

---

the Führer refuses to accept the gift because he has recently been given a new petrol lighter by Eva Braun. He orders the wooden horse burnt, and puffs contentedly on his pipe as it is consigned to the flames. All but two of the would-be assassins die from smoke inhalation. The survivors are then executed, and Hitler dances a pas-de-deux with Eva Braun to the fading sounds of Gotterdammerung as the end credits roll.

passed the journey by staring at the scenery unfolding slowly before me, and by trying to gain a little reassurance from stroking the fine leather of the suitcase which Herr Glissold had presented to me as a parting gift. It was a beautiful piece of luggage and had my name embossed in the hand-tooled leather, just below the Glissold crest of a boar and two sows rampant. Somehow, simply by feeling the quality of the leather and imagining the craftsmanship that had produced it, it became impossible to believe that the future could be other than civilised and safe. In my insecure state I took great comfort from that.

Herr Glissold could not accompany me on my journey from Schloss Streinevold, having a prior engagement to attend the wedding of the daughter of a local Burgher, so he had asked for my word of honour as a gentleman that I would deliver myself to Vilsbiburg for imprisonment. This was a parole that fettered me completely and denied me any chance of escape. Seething with frustration at my inability to cast off my moral manacles and strike out in the direction of England, I distracted myself on the train journey to the camp by eating alone in the dining car, where a moustachioed waiter tried with almost fanatical persistence to serve me with a light Hock even though our countries were now at war, a *faux pas* he seemed wilfully not to recognise.

After a wearying train ride of six hours, during which my ticket was punched an astonishing thirty-five times, I arrived at Vilsbiburg station to find a small contingent of German soldiers waiting to meet me. To my dismay, my new leather suitcase, containing the pyjamas, fresh towel and a monogrammed toiletries bag thoughtfully provided by Herr Glissold, was snatched from me the moment I stepped down on to the platform. A crowd of sturdy, moon-faced civilians had gathered to watch, and I noted that they became increasingly ugly as they took in my military uniform and the obvious quality of my luggage. One oafish-looking, muscular youth was carrying a small piglet in a kind of string papoose and he began to gesticulate with it obscenely, miming running it down with a bicycle and cracking its head with a blunt instrument (possibly a hammer) in what was obviously an attempt to unsettle me.

While the crowd whistled and jeered, an unpleasant-looking individual – whom I later came to know as Oberleutnant Krebbs – emptied my luggage on to the platform. He then ordered one of his subordinates to tear both arms from my new pyjamas and stamp them into some adjacent mud. His intention can have been only to humiliate me in front of the curious townspeople.

Stripped of all but my uniform I was then marched the twenty yards* or so to the gate of *Prolag 1* (*Vilsbiburg*) and told to sign in at the window of a small guard house. During this ceremony there was another unsophisticated attempt at humiliation when I was handed a small, blunted stump of pencil *in lieu* of a proper pen. Refusing to allow myself to be fazed, I simply nibbled the conical end until a small piece of lead was exposed, and then calmly signed my name with an air of superiority. This act of insubordination earned me a rifle butt to the kidneys, so I knew that my thrust had gone home.

Duly processed, I entered into the camp proper and nodded to the half dozen individuals I saw loitering within the tiny compound bounded by a tall perimeter fence. One or two nodded back, establishing the instant rapport of strangers meeting under difficult circumstances, but some – perhaps hardened by their wartime experiences – returned no more than surly scowls. I later discovered that they were Slovakian pipe-threaders who had become despondent at their imprisonment in a place which had no pipe.

From the guardhouse, a walk of less than three yards** brought me to the single building that dominated the centre of the compound, a one-storey barrack room measuring about thirty feet by fifteen†. Upon entering, I apprehended immediately how confined it was. Clearly our captors had not placed a high priority on comfort, with the vast majority of the internal space taken up by the sixteen bunk beds that lined the walls with

* Approximately 19 metres

** Approximately 2.7 metres

† Approximately 9 metres by 4 metres

scarcely a foot* of space between them. Down the length of the room, between the ends of the bunk beds, was a narrow aisle of some three feet** in width, along which numerous men ambled in an attempt to banish the monotony. Several others lay on bunks, reading, smoking or just staring vacantly at the rough-finished planks of the ceiling. One was systematically tearing small pieces from an old newspaper, rolling them into small balls, and attempting to flick them into the open mouth of a man sleeping in the next bunk, a sight that made me smile until the man awoke with a roar, mouth overflowing with thousands of small balls of paper, and began punching his tormentor repeatedly in the upper torso and throat. This was not to be the only time I witnessed extreme violence within the torturous existence we endured.

However many allied prisoners suffered far worse than I did, so details of the early days of my detention need not concern us here. Instead, I shall direct your attention to a curious event in the sixth month of imprisonment that was to prove a turning point with regard to my acquaintance with Selman-Troytt.

By March 1940 the camp had filled with a strong mix of inmates as our captors secured an increasing variety of prisoners from among numerous of the opposition forces which stood against their attempts to subjugate cultured nations. Besides the very small British contingent there was a smattering of Poles, two Frenchmen, some Czechs, a loose gathering of Serbians, a small but vocal bunch of Flems, and a large group of white-faced, hard-looking, thick-set individuals with eastern-Slavic features.

This latter group were by far the majority, and early attempts by the senior British officer, Colonel Hamish ('Scotty') McMurdo, to impose himself as the C.O. of the camp were rebuffed from outset. Chattering in a tongue incomprehensible to our ears, this majority group soon held a council of sorts at which one, a particularly coarse individual with

* Approximately 30 centimetres

** Approximately 90 centimetres

strangely tufted eyebrows and a heavily scarred face, emerged victorious after a short fight with a bald man who reminded me of an ink drawing of Genghis Khan that I had seen at school.

Brutish though the Slavs may have been, they were not to hold sway unimpeded, for many privates from the British ranks matched them in roughness, brute strength and coarseness; and so, over time, was forged an uneasy coalition that oversaw most matters pertaining to discipline and camp life.

The British contingent made several attempts to extend an olive branch to these other ethnic groups, but in large part our efforts were unrewarded. Many were surly, brooding brutes with a variety of skin conditions that one does not often see in England, and they had no English through which we might communicate with them. Even their names were largely unpronounceable, and after a while we were forced to concede that there was little we could do for them.

Given the supposedly temporary nature of our accommodation, our captors were not concerned with enforcing the segregation and classification of prisoners that would later define the identity of so many detention camps. *Prolag 1* (*Vilsbiburg*) became much more of a melting pot, holding a spread of inmates from across all services, regiments and nationalities. Thus it was that flying officers (such as Flight Lieutenant Bat ('Batty') Crang) might rub shoulders daily with ordinary sailors, whilst educated officers from good homes might be housed cheek-by-jowl with working class privates. This situation was far from ideal, as good discipline in the British armed services has relied always upon a strict segregation of ranks and classes, and Colonel McMurdo was quick to realise the worrying implications. Inevitably, following even such a short exposure to such conditions, familiarity began to breed contempt and respect began to diminish.

Another factor ignored by our captors was the need to impose a decent limit on inmate population, and the original maximum for which the hut was designed (32 prisoners) was quickly exceeded. As inmate numbers climbed to one hundred and fifty, so naturally did the appalling congestion within the tiny hut. There was nowhere to sit down, and the effect was not unlike standing for hours in a crowded elevator car, although when I made this comparison to my colleagues some said that they were reminded more of standing in a smoke-filled carriage on the London Underground during rush hour.

Living conditions within the hut were as unsanitary as one might imagine, and worsened day by day. The transmission of certain diseases accelerated when prisoners sleeping four or five to a bed became more common as the inmate population increased. British officers tried, as tactfully as possible, to segregate men so that those of similar class might sleep together, but their attempts were thwarted by a small group of large privates who insisted on sleeping wherever their fancy took them.

The northern end of the hut housed a wood stove, a slop bucket and a single cold-water tap, although neither of the latter were often utilised. It was only the most diligent or the most desperate prisoner who was willing to thrust aside the hostile crowds in order to perform his ablutions in open view. Very few were willing to sit on the bucket, and for those considering a wash there was no face cloth or towel. There was not even any soap. There had been a small cake early on but it was used as a soup thickener by some of the less fastidious. Those awaiting a turn at sleeping stood in dense, irascible crowds at the warmer end by the stove, or shivered in lines in the aisle between the bunk ends.

Conditions outside were no better. In addition to the often harsh weather, we had to contend with exercising up to one hundred and fifty men in a compound with barely enough space to accommodate thirty-two. Frankly put, there was not room enough, and eventually it was decided – principally by some brawny privates from the Durham Light Infantry in consultation with what may have been a Pole – that one half of the inmates would have to remain in the hut whilst the other went out for air. After one hour the shift would change, turn and turn about throughout a thirteen hour day, so that the hut was constantly emptying and refilling, with streams of men struggling to pass one another as they sought to enter or leave the hut by the single door. Finally, the congestion became so bad that we were separated into groups and were issued with small coloured tags that allowed us to ascertain where we were supposed to be at any specific time – whether in the hut, leaving the hut, outside the hut, or re-entering the hut.

There was one communal latrine – really no more than a flimsy outhouse – and reaching it from within the crowded hut often proved beyond the capability of inmates. Even supposing one were willing to brave the taunts and blows of other prisoners, particularly those immediately displaced by one's passage through the throng, one had still to negotiate the close-packed crowd outside and then wait in line at the latrine, often in freezing winter snow or blistering summer sun. Under such adverse conditions it is perhaps excusable that some men made other arrangements, making discreet use of a bottle, or sometimes a butter tin, and then carrying their cargo with them to be emptied on their next journey to the outside.

However, the Slavic contingent had no such qualms or niceties – or bottles – and its members were not above snatching a mug directly from the lips of another inmate and pressing it into service in front of companions who laughed heartily at the discomfiture of the owner into whose hands the vessel was then forcefully returned. Protestations could precipitate a violent altercation, so many suffered this indignity in silence.

The outlook from the camp was uninspiring, with only the northern end offering a view that was other than cinderblock, concrete or wooden walls. Staring through the northern fence, one had the railway tracks running laterally before one, a raised platform immediately beyond them, and then a row of commercial businesses that attracted a stream of visitors through the day. Rustic families came often to transact a variety of affairs, and while the children rushed into the pastry shop to consume as much confection as their Germanic mouths could hold, their mother might visit the butcher for sausage while their father carried a calf into the abattoir to be slaughtered. Later, the whole family might rendezvous at the blacksmith to buy some nails or have their boots re-shod with iron hoops.

I passed many hundreds of hours pressed against the fence, staring at the passing tide of rural humanity. I might see businessmen stepping gingerly over the effluvium flushed from the abattoir as they hurried to buy a train ticket, or young women in dirndls bargaining hard at the blacksmiths for wheel rims or leg braces. In retrospect, it may have been such interludes that kept me sane, for the sight of these everyday activities only five* yards away made me feel less alienated, the silence and overt hostility of the protagonists notwithstanding.

Not for us then the relative luxuries of certain other camps, which frequently boasted parade grounds, exercise areas, washing facilities, and even small 'gardening' areas. For us it was enough just to find space to breathe air that was not contaminated with the foul miasma of human waste, offal and hot iron.

I realise that I have neglected to describe in detail our sleeping conditions, but they will have to be conjectured. With one hundred and fifty men using sleeping accommodation designed for only thirty-two, the choice was stark and simple: the bunks had either to be shared or used in shifts. In fact both systems were employed as a matter of necessity, for no matter how comfortable any man felt with his immediate circle of companions, one tier of a bunk bed, measuring only some thirty inches** across, could not possibly accommodate the five men who might want to use it each night. There was simply not room enough for all occupants to sleep securely, especially those in an upper bunk who might shift in their sleep and find themselves plummeting onto the bodies of sleepers below.

Different solutions were tried, including men in the upper bunks lashing themselves to the framework with strips of blanket tied under their knees and arms, but one hour of this was reckoned to be the limit before discomfort overcame tiredness and made sleep impossible.

Eventually a compromise of sorts was reached, with men generally sleeping three to a bunk ('topping and tailing' or 'making spoons' to

---

* Approximately 4.5 metres

** Approximately 76cm

make more efficient use of the space) whilst the remaining forty percent of the inmates stood inside the hut in a tightly-packed group. Sleeping accommodation was allocated on a strict 'five-man' rota system, with men being spelled in hourly stages. Thus in any 'three man' bed the fourth (waiting) man would replace the first (sleeping) man after one hour, the fifth (waiting) would replace the second (sleeping) after two hours, and the first (now waiting) would replace the third (still sleeping) after three hours. The second (now waiting) would replace the fourth (now sleeping) an hour later, and by the time another hour had passed the third (now waiting) would replace the fifth (now sleeping), thereby ensuring that all three original members were back in the bed, albeit in a different order. In theory this gave each man two hours sleep but in practice it was less, for each sleeper had to contend with the disturbances of the shift changes as well as the noises of men scaling the upper bunks. To make matters worse, the shift changes could not be accommodated just once upon every hour because there was simply inadequate space for all the men to move around at the same time, so changeovers had to be staggered throughout each hour, with one sleeper relieving another somewhere in the hut every two minutes, thereby creating a sense of almost endless movement, rustling, quiet groans and frequent muffled oaths.

Such nights were lengthy and demoralising, but each dawn brought renewed hope, as well as a chance of being allowed to visit the latrine.

While it was an initial thrill to escape the confines of the hut, it should be emphasised that being outside in the compound (or *being out*, as we termed it) had drawbacks too. It was an undeniable improvement in terms of smell, but after the first few seconds it became as confined as within. With anything up to one hundred men in only some forty square yards* of space (allowing for the exclusion zone around the latrine and the ordure pit) we had no room to 'stroll' as such. However, due to the marginally increased shoulder room, men *were* able to move more easily than in the hut, as long as they did so in small groups

* 29.264 square metres

and synchronised their foot movements to a beat provided by the group leader.

Those men not in motion – which most people had to be, whether they desired it or not – were on the outer fringes and were pressed inevitably against the wire fencing, a position which became more and more uncomfortable as the day lengthened, particularly if a wire strand were pressing hard into one's cheeks or across the bridge of one's nose.

As groups and individuals circled slowly in the close-packed throng inside the compound, the gate guard, Hans von Stemper, would converse vigorously with whoever was passing closest to him. I dreaded absolutely those occasions when it was my turn. He was a fleshy, obese individual with pendulous lips and large jowls, who had reasonably good English and an absolute passion for cold meats. I cannot recall a single occasion when I saw him without a ham slice or a *wurst* of some kind, and while speaking he emitted a spray of tiny meat particles that rained unrelentingly on those he addressed.

His particular obsession was a Max Miller concert he had seen during a pre-war trip to Blackpool, and I can see him now, face only inches from mine, head bobbing and jaws chewing, as he showered me with a fine spray of partly masticated pork whist declaring: '*Ja Ja*, I am liking too much this Max Miller. Such good yokes'. He would then pose in what he considered to be an imitation of Miller and repeat: '"I have got ze best vife in Englund. Allzo I say it myself, the best vife in Englund. Ze ozzer vun iz in Africa!" Ha ha ha. I am liking too much your English humour. Ha ha ha.'

It was a revolting experience, the more so in hot weather because the sun tended to dry the meat flakes as soon as they made contact with the skin, so that those involved in a lengthy discourse with von Stemper built up a facial coating that resembled flock wallpaper. In an attempt at levity we called it 'being diStempered'*, but it was no laughing matter for apart from the obvious discomfort of such a crusty appendage in

* 'Distemper' was an early form of wall coating, usually made from powdered chalk or lime and size.

accommodation without washing facilities, this coating carried with it another danger insofar as it was not uncommon to awaken to find one's face being sucked by hungry colleagues desperate for a taste of meat.

I cannot recall precisely when I heard the first rumours of an escape attempt being planned, but I know that they lifted the spirits of every man, even those who had yet to realise that they were in captivity.

The rumours hardened into fact when an Escape Committee was formed one night after we had been locked into the hut. Around the stove the camp leaders began to make suggestions and plans as to how to gain our liberty, and word of their discussions was relayed in whispers the length and breadth of the hut. Colonel McMurdo straightaway moved to elect himself leader of the Escape Committee, but his campaign speech was silenced quickly by Private Haskins from Newcastle-under-Lyme, a bull-necked man with an absolutely huge and intimidating forehead. By means of several hand gestures he explained to the Colonel that he, Haskins, would be better suited to negotiate with our Slavic companions and would be better placed to prosecute the British position.

In consultation with the Slavic leadership, and in the absence of any other ideas, it was agreed that an escape would be attempted by tunnel. Several hours of heated dispute produced a plan.

The first tunnel, nicknamed 'Charlie' by the British but something entirely different by every other ethnic group, would go north from the stove, under the compound, the wire and the railway tracks, to emerge eight yards* later in the Vilsbiburg abattoir. Here, meat supplies would be obtained to fuel the second stage of the escape. Once heavily stocked with meat for the journey, each man would exit stealthily from the rear of the abattoir and head for Switzerland.

After heated debate, during which one combatant felt the full force of Haskins' extraordinary forehead, it was agreed that the tunnel would be dug by an international team consisting of Polish, Flemish, French and British tunnellers. The Slavs opted to reserve themselves for

---

* 7.3 metres

intelligence work, in particular the forging of the papers and documents so necessary to the safe flight through Germany of numerous escapees.

A second tunnel would go west from the latrine, under the ordure pit and the wire, to emerge two yards* later in a briar patch next to the empty grape silo. As a starting point for a tunnel, the latrine held several significant advantages. It was already very close to the wire fence, necessitating much less digging. It was also generally regarded as the last place that the enemy would expect a tunnel to begin, since it was daunting enough to enter the latrine for only minutes at a time, let alone work below it for hours. The only significant disadvantage we could identify was that such a tunnel would lead nowhere useful, emerging as it would in a closed and narrow alley that formed a perfect ambush point between two watchtowers. Anyone spotted leaving the tunnel would need to run the gauntlet of rapid machine-gun fire from both ends of the alley, thereby decreasing his chance of leaving the alley alive. Even assuming he made it past the northern watchtower, the escapee would still need to make a fast jinking run through a hail of bullets in order to try and gain Kaiser Wilhelm Strasse uninjured. Only at this point would he be able to relax and collect himself a little before setting off and finding his way to Switzerland undetected.

Lieutenant Arthur ('Ready') Salted suggested that it may be better tactically if the escape were effected in broad daylight so that the escapee, provided that he dodged the machine-gun fire, could try to evade detection by ducking into the pastry shop and mingling with the lunchtime crowd. Others disagreed, stating that it would be difficult for the escapee to blend in since his filthy clothes, his odour and his ragged breathing would mark him out from the other patrons dressed in freshly laundered dirndls and oiled lederhosen. Salted agreed readily, but replied that at least his suggestion afforded the escapee the opportunity to buy a meat pie before recapture. This generated much debate, but eventually it was decided that we were deviating from the main point

---

* 1.8 metres

and that the tunnel should first be dug and we would then concern ourselves with how to escape from it. The task of realising the latrine tunnel was assigned to four British officers, among them Flight-Lieutenants Jeffrey ('Daubs') Jamison and Penton ('Smears') Crane, the first two pilots shot down over Normandy! In a burst of British pluck and sardonic wit they nicknamed the tunnel 'Crust', in acknowledgement of the then condition of the ordure pit.

In preparation for the excavations, a survey of the camp was proposed by Lieutenant Jack ('Jack') Ganglia. Strictly speaking, a survey was not required as the distances were so short, but the escape committee felt that allowing Ganglia to undertake one might distract him from annoying fellows around him with his non-stop talking and other irritating habits. He had no surveying skills, as such, but set to work with great energy, measuring and pacing where possible. In lieu of a tape measure he used string, and he built a rudimentary theodolite from a butter tin, a piece of broken mirror and the lenses taken from someone's glasses while they slept. As tunnelling work proceeded he made extensive calculations, and then wrote up all his work on a blank page torn from the front of a communal bible. It was a beautiful piece of work, given the limitations

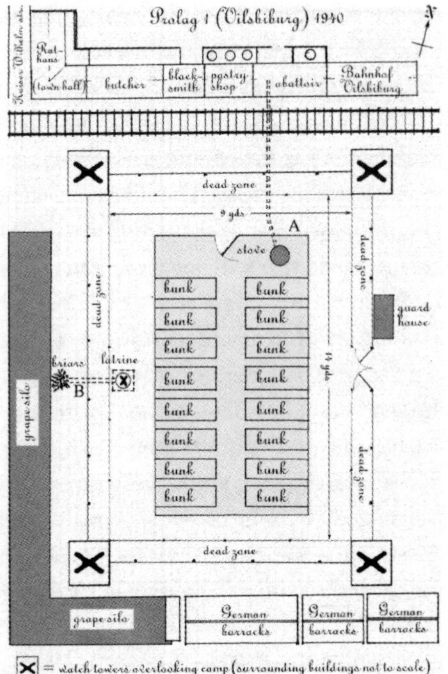

Drawn by Lt. Jack 'Jack' Ganglia, the escape committee's 'official' surveyor.
Reproduced by kind permission of the Ganglia family.

both of his tools and of intellect, and no less deserving of praise for being wholly unnecessary.

I had hoped for a place on 'Charlie' but found myself assigned to 'Crust'. As I had no experience with tools of any kind, I was given the job of lookout. Compared with the tasks that faced the tunnellers, mine was a reasonably light duty and involved standing in the latrine for six hours each day, keeping watch to ensure that no Germans came near it to discover the activities of those working beneath my feet. The work was tedious more than arduous, and I spent my days flapping my arms inside the latrine to try and maintain circulation in the chilly spring air.

My presence was not popular with those using the facility, which was cramped even before I took up my observation post inside the flimsy plywood box, but it was essential to the mission so we did our best to ignore each other while they went about their ministrations as I peered out fixedly through cracks in the walls.

Luck favoured the 'Crust' team, in that the earth was already considerably softened and the tunnel, at only two yards* in length, needed no shoring up. The tunnel was finished in less than a week, to the profound relief of those inmates who had found it too embarrassing to visit the latrine with me present in the cubicle.

With 'Crust' completed and 'Charlie' already past the halfway point, discussion turned increasingly to the logistics of escape. Initially we had proposed that each escapee should carry with him a full set of forged but authentic-looking documents. However, this plan was abandoned with reluctance when it became clear that we were without assets such as paper, ink, forgery expertise, or original documents from which copies could be made. Finally, necessity being the mother of invention, it was agreed that each man would leave without documentation and would, if questioned by anyone, pretend to be mentally defective.

A similar compromise was reached with clothing. We had among the British contingent a former tailor, Lieutenant Montague ('Semite')

* 1.82 metres

Levine, who had initially proposed forming a sewing circle that would make alterations to our uniforms to render them less conspicuous. However, further analysis showed his plan to be unworkable as he was without needles, thread, scissors or cloth, or even enough space for members of his group to separate themselves by more than three inches. Finally, as a desperate last resort, it was suggested that each man would forcefully remove the insignia, lapels and collar of his immediate neighbour to produce a kind of ragged jerkin, such as mendicants might wear if they were suffering severely reduced cerebral capability. The marks from old insignia would be covered with ashes from the stove, rubbed well into the material to form a shiny patina of filth. It was not as much of a transformation as we would have wished, but it was the best we felt was possible under the circumstances.

As 'Charlie' neared completion it was decided that some kind of pictorial record of our appalling conditions should accompany us in order that the British High Command could lodge a formal complaint with their German counterparts. After much discussion it was decided that 'Slippy' Quilty, aided by Bat Crang, should undertake the daring exploit of rendering a facsimile of the camp from outside it.

Some of you will remember Captain P.T.F.E. ('Slippy') Quilty, since he was already a celebrated artist before he decided to lay aside his paint brush and assist the war effort. 'Slippy' had, before the war, exhibited at five consecutive 'retrospectives' at the Dudley and District Municipal Portrait Gallery quite near to his family's country seat, and all had received much publicity. His abstract piece 'Stained Velvet in Moonlight' had become a *cause celèbre* in Wolverhampton, while 'Thing on a Bed – paint on paper' was met with confusion by all who saw it. His agent was none other than Francisco Coroletti, the art expert famously rejected by Picasso as an 'armless bore without a scintilla of sense in his whole body'. Furious at the injustice of the comment, 'Slippy' was determined upon a post-war career that would eclipse Picasso's and enable him to force the artist into a public retraction and a written admission that Coroletti had arms.

In order to get them outside the fence, it was decided that our artistic team should join the small group of Polish inmates who were forcibly taken out each day for track maintenance work. Their fellow prisoners did their best to disguise them in readiness for the deception. To make them appear more Polish they first gave them a very uneven haircut, with the fringe on an oblique slant and small ragged tufts created all over the scalp. Then each was given a capacious pair of trousers to wear. Finally, they were coached on the crab-like gait and facial grimacing that were fundamental parts of the Polish bearing.

At 10.00 hours the following day the small Polish work detail, complete with its two impostors, was force-marched, crouching slightly, the eleven yards* to the front of the train station. Its escort of two armed guards took up position on the elevated platform while the workers were spread out on the line below. They were given small wire brushes with which to shine both rails. It was degrading, soul-destroying work, made infinitely worse by their inability to raise a satisfactory shine on the pitted surfaces. Moreover, at regular intervals it was necessary for all workers to leap from the track to avoid being injured by fast trains that arrived with little warning.

Those of us left inside the congested yard pressed our faces to the northern boundary wire and watched intently. As minutes ticked by we saw that 'Slippy' and Bat were inching further east along the track and away from the guards, past the abattoir and the Bahnhof ticket office, their movements covered by small diversions from their Polish colleagues.

Once past the ticket office, still bent double, they edged to their left until they were hidden from the guards by the corner of the building. At this point 'Slippy' moved up surreptitiously behind the hunched-over figure of Bat Crang and arched forward over him. After a whispered consultation I saw Bat carefully loosen his belt whilst 'Slippy' began to ease Bat's trousers down over his hips. While 'Slippy' was thus engaged, Bat salivated silently into his palm and slowly slid his hand back between his legs.

---

* Approx. 10 metres

I watched, trembling like a leaf. I risked a glance at the guards but saw they were pre-occupied, one in gnawing at a piece of very hard cheese and the other in monitoring his comrade's progress. Neither had noticed that our intrepid comrades were no longer in view. My attention returned to 'Slippy' because I was intent upon trying to fathom his exact purpose. There was something about the scene that I found troubling, but I was unable to put my finger on it.

I was still wholly perplexed as I saw 'Slippy' ease Bat's trousers to just below his buttocks. With deft movements he then reached into his own trousers and withdrew something that caused a collective intake of breath from my watching colleagues. It was nothing less than a crude 'stylus' he had fashioned ingeniously from a pigeon feather and a splinter of wood. He began softly dabbing it into Bat's palm, in which I later discovered was a thick-ish 'ink' made from a mixture of saliva and soot from the cinders. I was filled with an overpowering sense of admiration for two men prepared to put themselves in such a position, even though it was still not clear to me what their position was.

Then, with his hands held down surreptitiously at waist height, 'Slippy' began to draw! Of course he had no paper, but with swift and precise strokes he began sketching a facsimile of the camp on the tail of Bat's shirt. I was almost overcome, so great was my pride at their initiative, and nearly alerted the guards to their activity by shouting 'Bravo!' Fortunately, I managed to restrain myself at the last instant.

'Slippy' worked with accuracy and rapidity. It was a bravura performance, brought to a premature finish by the arrival of a train of gaping passengers. With their view of the camp blocked, our artists had no option but to adjust their dress and make their way back into the work party, 'Slippy' fuming with frustration at the inconvenient arrival of the train. Later he complained bitterly that he had not had a chance to finish the cross-hatching in places, and had been forced to leave out the surrounding buildings and all the inmates crushed inside the wire. He was also unhappy with the perspective, which he complained had been skewed by the undulations of Bat's buttocks. But all this was really no more than his artistic perfectionism at work for, really, the sketch was first-rate.

That night, in the hut, we clustered around Bat as he lowered his trousers to a collective sigh of admiration from the congregation, and I marvelled at the near-perfect representation of the exterior of the hell we called 'home'. To us it was much more than a piece of bravely obtained utilitarian intelligence: it was a thing of terrible beauty that seemed to capture our desolation in every tortured stroke.

Capt. P.T.F.E. Quilty (1918-1947) *Prolag 1 (Vilsbiburg) Exterior*, Ink on shirt
Reproduced by kind permission of the Quilty Family Trust

It was decided quickly at senior level that the picture could not be left *in situ* lest it become further soiled or creased. Bat stood cheerfully and stoically at attention whilst he sacrificed the lower back portion of his shirt to some judicious ripping by the Frenchmen. The precious picture was first rolled up and then, for further protection, wrapped inside a whole shirt taken from a Flem without his cooperation. The whole cargo was then hidden in the rafters to await passage with an escapee, and later presentation to the British authorities. However, owing to logistical difficulties it remained there until removed by the British in 1947*, at which point, because it was considered of no value to British intelligence, the war having ended,

* The camp was not liberated until well after the end of WWII.

it was presented to 'Slippy's' family as a fitting memorial to the man and his talent.

Those of you who wish to see the picture can do so, for it is housed now in the Imperial War Museum, on permanent loan from the Quilty family. I have visited it several times, and can never look at it without tears in my eyes, as well as a recollection of the fear and confusion I felt at what Quilty and Crang were doing. They were two of the most wonderful and fondly remembered colleagues I ever knew.* (Thus do such sad memories of terrible tragedies counterbalance the ineffable joys of our freedom.)

But I digress.

'Charlie' was finished in short order, with the tunnel bypassing the foundations of the station platform and abattoir and connecting directly with the offal drains through which we hoped to make good our escape.

By now we were desperate to leave. Many believed that the animals in the abattoir were treated better than we were, an assessment that was perhaps not wholly accurate, but it was certainly the case that our conditions were appalling. Many inmates had not removed any clothing since the previous autumn, and everyone dreaded to think what consequences the summer heat might bring.

Privates Haskins and Warnock conferred with other members of the escape committee and fixed the following Tuesday as the night of the proposed escape. It was the dark of the moon and suited our purposes admirably. Volunteers were called for, and one hundred and forty-two men raised their hands without hesitation. Another seven were volunteered by close friends since they were deemed unfit to decide for themselves, having little or no idea where they were.

That left only Major Clive ('Creamy') Butters, who had suffered from rapidly worsening myopia since colliding with a gate-post upon

* "Tragically, Bat 'bought it' unexpectedly when he fell beneath the wheels of the ambulance carrying him to the British Military Hospital in the first few hours of our liberation. 'Slippy' Quilty was mistaken for a spy and shot during a routine debriefing session in 1947." [*Taken from footnotes in the original edition. Ed.*]

arrival. It had caught him a tremendous blow between the eyes, the impact of which seemed to have dislodged his eyes from their normal track, for they became increasingly skewed as days passed. Close friends monitored his progress and reported that both eyes were travelling slowly inwards and upwards, apparently irrevocably. It was felt to be only a matter of time before the pupils disappeared from view completely.

One of the Frenchmen, Jacques ('Plantagenet') LaFunge, was convinced that the impact had made Butters acutely short-sighted, for LaFunge was able to get a sharp pin within a half inch of Butters' eyes before he suddenly screamed in panic and curled into a foetal position. Certainly his balance seemed affected, for he wove alarmingly on even the shortest journey, sometimes circling repeatedly until forced to his knees by friends.

The Flems were for abandoning Butters in the hut, feeling that he would jeopardize the escape by stumbling about in the abattoir, but his good friend Captain Simon ('Damask') Lint intervened, and stated emphatically that he and Butters would leave as a team, roped together as one man, with Butters tethered to his waist. We all applauded his loyalty, although Butters complained bitterly at this treatment for his pride would never allow him to admit that anything was amiss with his sight. Aiding him in his self-deception seemed a small kindness, so whenever he claimed to have 'the vision of a very young hawk' we all concurred clamorously, doing our best all the while to steer him away from sharp edges.

With Butters taken care of, we were then split into two groups, the proposal being that the main contingent of one hundred and twenty men would escape through 'Charlie' whilst a smaller force of thirty men would try to exit silently through 'Crust'. It was at this very point that a shortcoming of 'Crust' became apparent, for we suddenly noted that we would have no access to the tunnel during the dark of the moon, it being situated outside in the latrine and we being locked up in the hut during the night. This revelation caused several bitter complaints from the British tunnellers, during which the Slavs were insensitive enough to nudge each other and laugh, and otherwise have sport at the expense of the whole 'Crust' team who had worked so hard in difficult conditions. Reluctantly, 'Crust' was abandoned and all escapees routed via 'Charlie'.

By the following Tuesday we were wracked with nerves. The escape was set for midnight. By 1900 hours we had all eaten our evening soup ration and been squeezed back inside the hut. Over the next thirty minutes we ripped lapels, collars and insignias wherever they were visible, and then rubbed soot into any material we encountered around our bodies. The effect was mixed, although we certainly no longer resembled prisoners of war when we had finished. Each man was dressed in a shirt, and sometimes also an undershirt unless it had been stolen by someone now wearing two undershirts. A very ragged jerkin, often sleeveless, and billowing trousers of indeterminate origin and colour completed each man's habiliments. The whole ensemble was covered with new patches of encrusted grime that supplemented the old grime already collected since incarceration began. Hair, where still present, was tidied and smoothed flat to the head, where it was cemented in place by its own sebaceous pomade. We no longer looked like prisoners of war, but even the most optimistic among us could not ignore the fact that we did not look like typical German civilians. All in all, it was considered a blessing that we were hoping to travel by night.

With several hours to go, it was suggested that we get whatever rest we could to prepare ourselves for a sleepless and arduous night. I was lucky enough to be allocated bed space in the first sleeping shift, and drifted off dreaming about handling the pork stored in the abattoir.

When I awoke it was to a strange sense that something was different, but at first I could not place it. Then it occurred to me with a rush that what I was hearing was actually an *absence* of noise. With a start I jerked into a sitting position and found myself alone in a completely empty hut. I turned my head from side to side, marvelling at the freedom of being able to look along the whole ten yards* of the hut, and

---

* 9.14 metres

revelled in the luxury of being able to breathe air that had not been just expelled from the mouth of a fellow prisoner.

With a second violent start I realized that my comrades had forgotten to wake me. Their oversight seemed incomprehensible, as I had left specific instructions with sixteen of them to awaken me in time for the escape; but then it came to me that such replication could have been my undoing, for it might have easily occurred to each of them that one of the others would have taken care of the task. With a cry of alarm I jolted upright from a lower bunk and raced to the stove which was still lying on its side, exposing the tunnel mouth beneath its base. Although the pale daylight now creeping through the encrusted windows of the hut told me that my companions must have left many hours before, I was optimistic enough to put my head into the tunnel mouth and give a loud *halloo!* My voice bounced back to me, accompanied by a strong smell of fat and animal offal.

Unfortunately, Oberleutnant Krebbs chose that very moment to unlock the hut door to summon everyone for morning roll call and was aghast to discover an all but empty room with me kneeling by the only means of egress. In short, my captors reviewed the circumstantial evidence and arrived at the preposterous notion that I had been responsible both for the tunnel itself and for organizing the mass escape of one hundred and forty-nine prisoners through it. As a punishment I was sentenced to one month's solitary confinement, which in essence meant returning me to the hut as there was no one else in it. Later, as new arrivals began to trickle in to the camp, I was made to stand in the latrine, unless it was in use, in which case I was made to stand back in the hut. If both hut and the latrine were in use then I was made to stand in the corner of the yard. Eventually, all three locations again became occupied constantly and my sentence was commuted as it was no longer practicable to enforce it. But I anticipate myself.

For the first few days alone I tried to accustom myself to the space around me. It was so strange to be able to see the inner walls of the hut. And the floor, normally obscured by hundreds of ruined feet in flapping shoes, was covered with a veritable sea of nail parings and skin detritus which yielded an assortment of treasures thought lost forever. In one corner I found a partially dissolved fruit pastille that may well have fallen from the open mouth of a sleeping man, while near the slop bucket I found Captain Dearborn's truss. The first I ate with relish; the latter I stored away against a future emergency.

As time passed I received tid-bits of intelligence as to the fortunes of the escapees. All had made it through the abattoir, each having made sure to take off with a good supply of meat to sustain him on the journey. Of necessity, some had formed into teams of two or three so they could carry off a heavy side of beef or a whole ox carcass between them. Their food supply assured, they then fled in all directions, each man having his own firm opinion as to the likely location of Switzerland.

Some were quickly recaptured in local towns and villages, weighed down by more meat than their emaciated legs could carry, their attempts at appearing demented too amateurish to convince a suspicious populace. In ones and twos they filtered back into the camp, their countenances bearing ample evidence of mistreatment. All had black eyes and some were missing teeth. Sergeant Swooler was missing an entire top set, but still counted the loss worthwhile for the chance to have eaten meat right up until the very instant of his capture. With pride and excitement he recounted how he had stuffed the last of his meat rations into his mouth, refusing to yield them up when ordered to do so, thereby forcing his guards to smash his teeth out with a rifle butt in order to retrieve the last pieces of scrag-end he had yet to swallow.

Although forbidden to speak to me, a few men did whisper the odd word of encouragement as they passed. Lieutenant Simon ('Anchovy') Herring was kind enough to put my mind at rest by whispering: 'Message from Bat and Co. Left before they remembered you. All said to say "Sorry" if I saw you again. Knew you'd understand. Heads like sieves. Good men otherwise. Top drawer.'

Lint returned alone, with only a frayed rope end to show where he had once been linked to Butters. He was distinctly reticent about the affair, and threatened to punch anyone who enquired directly as to Butters' whereabouts.

'Slippy' Quilty returned curiously chastened by the experience. He had left a flamboyant extrovert who often burst into song in the middle of the night, but returned a timid loner who would look no one in the eye directly. At night we saw his body shudder as he wept silently when he thought himself unobserved.

Bat Crang was returned to us bound and transported roughly in a motorcycle sidecar. Obviously the victim of a sound thrashing, his round, cheery face was unrecognizable under the welter of contusions that disfigured it. Some of them never disappeared, lending his head an uneven appearance, not unlike a distended football at the moment a hardened toecap makes contact with it. Yet, brave to the end, he maintained a fusillade of jokes and wisecracks that made others laugh and which tempted the more compassionate men to overlook his appearance and allow him into their conversations

One drawback of the escape plan, unforeseen during the discussion stages, was that those who had given very convincing portrayals of witless mendicants had been taken up as the real thing and were now languishing in local asylums. To date [*1951 - Ed.*] none has been released despite the intervention of their respective governments, so they would have been better off staying in the hut until 1947. But of course we know that now only with the benefit of hindsight.

The fate of many others remains a mystery. From my own post-war researches I have failed to uncover any traces of many escapees, including Colonel McMurdo, Privates Warnock and Haskins, and a host of other courageous man who did their best to frustrate the Nazi battle lust in the early part of the war. Of the original one hundred and forty-nine escapees, only twenty-two were ever returned to *Prolag 1* (*Vilsbiburg*) and almost none of the meat was recaptured. But I digress.

I recall that it was on a fine, sunny day in May 1940, some two months after the escape attempt, that Flight-Lieutenant Angstrom entered the camp. He was a tall, willowy, fresh-faced young officer with a patrician nose, immensely compact lips and the smallest ears I had ever seen. Each was about the size of a half-crown, and the skin had the texture of a walnut. I wanted to ask him if they were the result of a birth defect, but it was hard to introduce the subject into a conversation without appearing boorish. He was diffident to the point of complete silence, and endured the joshing and ritualistic de-bagging from his fellow prisoners with obvious discomfort.

With only fifty-two inmates in residence at that time there was even room for a few of us to sit down inside or outside the hut, and thus it was that I encountered Angstrom seated in a patch of pale spring sunshine, his thin back pressed onto the fencing and a large volume open on his knees. Books were an unheard of luxury prior to the escape, but several volumes had been allowed in with the recent intake of prisoners.

Angstrom intrigued me, and I was determined to try to communicate with him if possible; but it was difficult to begin, for we had not been formally introduced since his arrival and he gave me no encouragement by word or gesture. Indeed my conversational openings were met with an averted gaze and complete silence, and when I inquired as to what he was reading he stared fixedly at the ground before slowly lifting the book so that I could read the title on the spine. I could see that the volume was entitled *A Study of Seepage*, and that it was authored by Jeremy Selman-Troytt. Neither title nor author meant anything to me at the time, but my questions about the book proved an excellent opening gambit. Gradually, Angstrom overcame his reticence and began to speak, haltingly at first and then with increasing animation as the light of enthusiasm began to shine in his young eyes.

He spoke of his passion for the man's work, encountered at first when he had stumbled across *Reflections on Skin – A Study of Intensive Flaking* at his college library in Cambridge and was instantly caught up by the author's verve and élan. He wanted more, but Selman-Troytt's works were then long out of print and hard to find. By scouring second-hand bookshops he built an impressive personal collection, including the very rare *My Blood – What It Is and Why I Need It*, and was seldom without a volume of the man's work close at hand thereafter.

When he surrendered his uncompleted degree to join the RAF, he broke King's regulations by removing his parachute from inside its packing and replacing it with treasured Selman-Troytt volumes, so desperate was he to continue his study of the man's work in the event he should be shot down and captured.

When he *was* actually shot down it occurred to him, just before bailing out of the stricken aircraft, that far from being equipped with a life-saving parachute he was weighed down by an additional three stones* in the form of twelve hardbound editions of Selman-Troytt's earlier work. In those few seconds, as he hovered between life and death, he was faced with the type of dilemma that confronts many of us at one time or another in our lives. In a desperate attempt to resolve it, he snatched the parachute from the co-pilot and jumped from the burning 'plane, his arms tightly around his treasured books in an effort to cushion them from harm.

They nearly proved his undoing, for they hastened his descent and the additional frontal weight caused him to rotate slightly forward so that he landed face down, fracturing ankles, elbows, chin and nose. Unable to walk, crawl or eat, he lay motionless for three days until found by wandering peasants who ransacked his possessions while he lay disabled. Illiterate even in their own language, they had no respect for the written word in English and a number of pages from *A Catalogue of Tumescence* (1873–1898) were pressed into service as fire-lighting spills and lavatory paper. This desecration becomes even more disturbing when one considers the financial loss, for an undamaged copy of *A Catalogue of Tumescence* (1873–1898) fetched 1800 guineas at Sotheby's in 1949, making it the most expensive lavatory paper in history!

As our relationship bloomed by the fence, Angstrom allowed me to examine the other volumes for which he had sacrificed so much mobility in his joints. All were expensively bound and substantial in size, the smallest being some nine hundred pages in length. The largest contained two thousand eight hundred and seventy-three pages!

---

* 19kg

My eye was caught by two titles in particular: *The First Time I Soiled My Trousers* and *My Seventh Nocturnal Emission*. Intrigued, I settled down to read the first, and as page followed page I experienced something of an epiphany, for it came as a staggering revelation to find the commonplace made special in such a way. As I became more excited I realised that Selman-Troytt had a unique talent for taking everyday events – occurrences that we all took for granted – and then thrusting them before a reader's eyes with a scientist's talent for examination and evaluation. Yet his revelations were not dry and academic, but couched in a readable style that was warm, understanding and, most important of all, *human*! In our camp, for example, men were soiling themselves every day, yet who would have thought to examine such an occurrence from a scientific point of view? Certainly none of us prisoners, for soilings were experiences we expected without thought: a fundamental part of normal existence!

And from the commonplace to the rare, the epiphany continued unabated with *My Seventh Nocturnal Emission*. I too had once experienced a nocturnal emission of my own but, trapped in a bubble of my own self loathing, had considered myself alone. Suddenly, with Selman-Troytt's own experiences held before me, I felt freed. Almost cleansed.

Excitedly, I pressed Angstrom for more details about the man, but what little he knew served only to whet my appetite further. It seemed that his publications had been suppressed by his family following his death in 1916. Since then his extant works had languished on dusty shelves, forgotten and neglected as the world raced onward towards televisual transmission and trans-Atlantic air travel. Yet as the world rushed to embrace this red-hot technology, I saw in a flash that we were simultaneously starving ourselves of the food we needed to calm the spirit and feed the mind. Instantaneously, I saw that Selman-Troytt could be the force that succoured a legion of lost and frightened men in a world of increasing uncertainty and insecurity; a beacon of hope in a world of casual and indiscriminate brutality, where human beings were seen as increasingly worthless and where machines would certainly sweep us from the face of the earth one day.

At that very moment I determined that I would form a Selman-Troytt Appreciation Society* as soon as the war ended, and through it I would try to disseminate the author's findings and observations, as well as undertake research to establish more about the background of the man himself.

Scarcely able to contain myself, I leapt to my feet and ran into the hut

[Remainder omitted. Ed.*]*

* See p.248 for details of the Selman-Troytt Appreciation Society (S.T.A.S.).

Appendix II

Very little of Selman-Troytt's early adolescent correspondence survives, principally because many missives went undelivered by a postal service unable to discern any addressees in the irregular loops with which the envelopes were covered. Those few that were delivered were invariably consigned to the fire by recipients who had no idea of the sender's identity and could make no sense of the contents.

Below is an extremely rare exception from 1879. It was sent to the Bishop of Leicester at his London address, and arrived only because it was hand-delivered to the Bishop's home on the other side of Berkeley Square. It was then retained only because the Bishop believed the contents to be an encoded warning or threat, and had the letter sent to Lambeth Palace for examination. There it survived only because it was misfiled under 'Pending Lawsuits' and was not discovered again for nearly one hundred years.

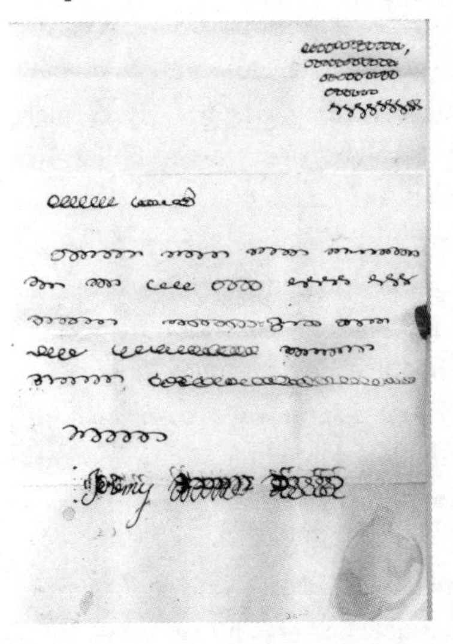

The letter now forms part of the *Selman-Troytt Collection* at the Selman-Troytt Appreciation Society (S.T.A.S.), although a facsimile is available to view at their headquarters.

Appendix III(a)

rchival study suggests that the account which influenced Selman-Troytt so profoundly was the following:

. . . but Hugo refused upon every occasion, using the excuse that it was unsanitary. His friend Rochemel, a man of fastidious nature and proper habits, was even more dilatory. He expressed the deepest repugnance at the prospect of touching his genitals, and refused to retract his foreskin despite the clamorous exhortations of family members and medical experts.

Instead he contrived an engine of various working parts, levers, and pulleys which, when positioned by his side, could offer a rubber-tipped clamp to the offending prepuce. Rochemel squeezed a rubber bulb with his left hand (the resulting air pressure acting upon the clamp and causing it to close in a controlled fashion) while his right hand clasped a perpendicular lever – not unlike a locomotive points-switching lever – connected by a cantilever to the control arm and moving the clamp through an arc of thirty-five degrees on a horizontal plane. By virtue of his excellent hand-to-eye co-ordination Rochemel was able to retract the foreskin within a short period. His fastest time was recorded at Arles: seven minutes and forty-nine seconds.

The contrivance was mounted upon castors to aid manoeuvrability, was cylindrical in appearance, and was possessed of two handles on the upper portion. Its total weight was a little over thirty-four kilos. Rochemel was very proud of his workmanship, and would frequently give demonstrations to enraptured audiences. On one occasion he was invited to an audience with King Gustav where, rumour has it, the King attempted to retract his own foreskin but found the task beyond him.

Extract from Montmartre to Pigalle by Way of Arles *by Henri Terchad, 1876 – translated by Simon Branchard, New Court Press, London, 1881.*

Despite rumours suggesting the contrary, many of which were started by Rochemel himself, he never succeeded in getting the weight of his floor-standing model below thirty-two kilos, considerably in excess of Selman-Troytt's maximum target weight of twenty-four kilos for a portable version. Nor did Rochemel ever succeed in making his own contrivance portable, again despite persistent rumours of a breakthrough prototype.

By 1885, orders for Rochemel's floor-standing prepuce retractor were beginning to dry up as many would-be purchasers became impatient with its weight and with the inconvenience of using a retractor that was not attached to one's body. To make matters worse, Rochemel had failed to patent the original, so pirated copies of inferior quality began to flood into France from countries where labour markets were cheap. Many were poorly made from rough cast iron and were considerably heavier than Rochemel's own machine; but they were often confused with his product and thus served to dilute his reputation even further. Some even caused accidents, as the shoddy castors upon which they were transported were often unequal to the task of supporting the extra weight and sometimes snapped or shattered, causing the retractor to fall sideways without warning. If this happened while the machine was in use then considerable damage could be caused to the glans, and Rochemel was threatened with several lawsuits by customers whose genitals had been injured or lost in such incidents.

By 1896 he was a broken man, living in poverty in a Parisian tenement in one of the city's less salubrious districts. His final days were spent in a fog of alcoholism, his spasmodic periods of lucidity used for demonstrations of the machine that had been so much a part of his earlier life and fame; but it was clear to all observers that his heart was not in them. One contemporary remarked: 'There was just no excitement in him any more, no zest, no *joie-de-vivre*. He often seemed to lose his way in mid-manoeuvre, or become distracted, and then he would stop and gaze out of the window as though seeing back into the past. On one occasion he seemed to forget what he was doing altogether and after twenty minutes of inactivity a friend stepped forward out of compassion and quietly repacked his genitals for him. His co-ordination was slower too. I don't think he ever made a sub-ten-minute retraction during all the time he was in Paris.' Rochemel died shortly before this account was recorded.

He and Selman-Troytt never met, and although Selman-Troytt was quite ready to admit to the influence that Rochemel had had upon his own research there is absolutely no question of plagiarism. Although both men were attempting to resolve the same issue, they were approaching the problem from wholly different directions. Selman-Troytt was never interested in producing a prepuce retractor 'at any price', a criticism often levelled at Rochemel, and thus was unwilling to make the same concessions that Rochemel did. His radically different philosophy can be summed up best by a statement made to a journalist from *The Illustrated London News* in 1902, following a disappointing public trial of his latest prototype: 'It simply has to be made portable. That may be the most technically demanding route to follow, but it has to be portable . . . or it should not be made at all!'

As an interesting footnote, Selman-Troytt held no patent for his proposed designs and *had no intention of ever applying for one*. He had no desire for wealth, and no wish to profit from work that he regarded as being of benefit to mankind in general and men in particular. Instead he wanted the instrument to pass into the hands of the needy with minimum delay and for minimal outlay. As Guscott confirmed at a press conference after Selman-Troytt's funeral in 1916: 'He dreamed of little else than a prepuce retractor carried on every back.'

Appendix III(b)

Before & After

Selman-Troytt's Journal Notes for August 18th 1885 record his attempts to realise an illustration of Rochemel's floor-standing prepuce retractor. Jeremy was only seventeen at the time, and his attempts at draughtsmanship are correspondingly poor and ill-executed. However the sketch (below left) was precious to him and remained by his side until a replacement could be produced.

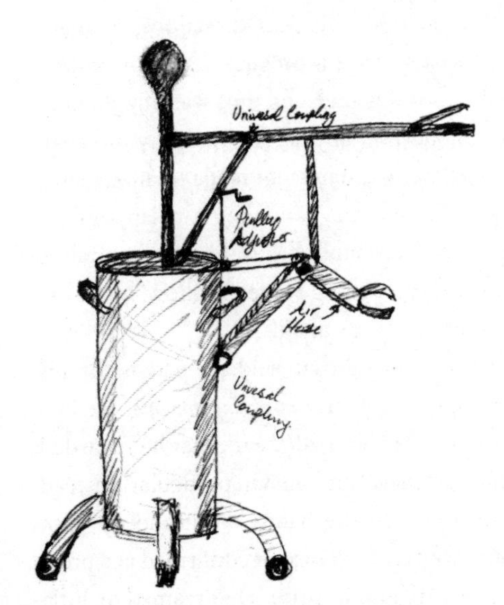

At the age of twenty-one, Selman-Troytt came into his inheritance, a trust fund set aside for his future by his mother Lady Bethany, and immediately invested the whole of it in obtaining a more accurate representation of the floor-standing retractor. He commissioned Jennings & Evincourt, the engineers with whom he would subsequently forge a strong bond over many years, to produce professional images that would inspire further refinements.

They based their drawing on Selman-Troytt's original and worked closely with him to realise the image he held in his mind. Six new drawings were produced in total, of which only one (left) survives. Note the different site of the pulley adjuster, a refinement upon which Selman-Troytt had laboured during the intervening years.

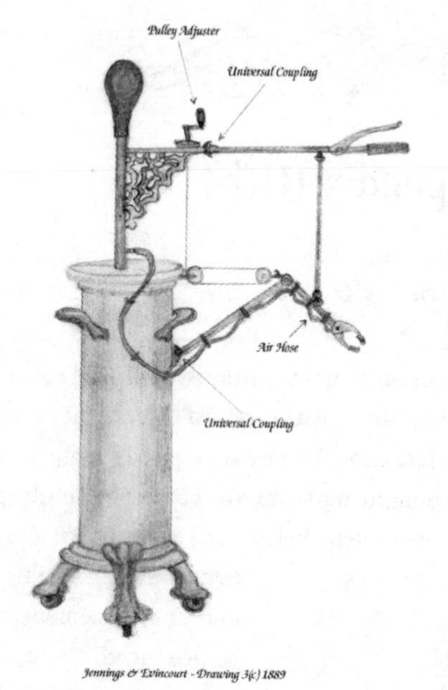

Jennings & Evincourt - Drawing 3(c) 1889

Although he had no intention of trying to produce a floor-standing model, Selman-Troytt's efforts to understand its mechanical complexities were the foundation upon which his designs for a *portable* retractor were based. He often referred to the illustrations below as 'inspirational'.

Appendix III(c)

Very few of Selman-Troytt's own sketches survive. By his own admission he was a better descriptive writer than a graphic artist (he had extremely limited manual dexterity and very poor hand-to-eye coordination) and preferred to express his ideas in technical and academic prose. Furthermore, as his requirements were invariably for highly specified and accurate technical drawings, he chose to leave them in the hands of experts. However from time to time he would complete preliminary sketches which professionals could use for initial guidance.

This exciting example is from the margin of his journal dated January 11th 1897 and clearly shows that he intended the portable prepuce retractor to accommodate a top hat so that it could be worn at formal functions.

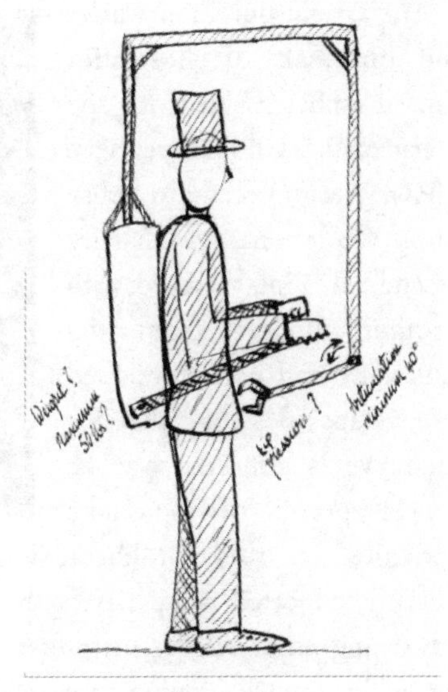

The annotations are as follows from left to right:

Weight?
Maximum 50 lbs?
Tip pressure?
Articulation minimum 40°

Appendix IV

The Selman-Troytt Appreciation Society (S.T.A.S.)

The Selman-Troytt Appreciation Society was founded in 1948 by Finlay Finlayson (below), who enjoyed the distinction of being the longest serving inmate in a German P.O.W. camp. He was captured on the first day of WWII when, lost and confused, he landed his surveillance aircraft in what he believed was Switzerland in order to ask for directions. Unfortunately he had miscalculated his position and was actually on the outskirts of Stuttgart.

His arrival only hours after the outbreak of hostilities caused embarrassment for the Germans who did not yet have a P.O.W. camp ready to house him. While one was hastily assembled, Finlay stayed with brother officers from the Luftwaffe and here developed friendships so strong that for many years after the war he was suspected of espionage activities. He was not liberated until late in 1947, his small and obscurely located camp having been overlooked completely by the advancing allies during their first, second, and third offensives. He passed his time fashioning chess sets from candle-wax.

Although plainly still exhibiting the after-effects of malnutrition, he is shown here proudly wearing his '*de-mob*' suit at the inaugural meeting of the Society.

The Society he founded is dedicated to researching and republishing the extant writings of Jeremy Selman-Troytt, and to compiling biographical details on those family members and acquaintances who may have influenced his work.

*'Working with the S.T.A.S. – Recollections of a Wonderful Career'**
by
Marichal Pincent-Vestry (Miss)

I remember my first day at work so well. It was a beautiful summer's morning in 1949 and the Kensington air was thick with the smell of hyacinths and dogwood as I left our London townhouse for the short walk to the tube. It was wonderful to feel the sun on my face again after it had been away so long, although I groaned inwardly at the thought that my face would soon be brushed with freckles! In those days, of course, make-up was still very hard to obtain, so we had little that we could use to cover blemishes or conceal such imperfections as any

* Published first in *Women's Trifles*, Issue 29, pp. 37–56, 1974, Arctic Publications, Stoneygate Mews, Rotherham. *Women's Trifles* began in 1911 but ceased publication in its own right in 1978, when it was re-named *Trifles* in keeping with a more feminist agenda and the non-gender -specific demands of the market. Shortly after, it was re-named *Tittle* in an attempt to compete with more progressive competitors like *Cosmopolitan*. More re-brandings – *Tattle*, *Tittle Tattle*, *Irrelevancies*, *Cooking For Love*, *(How To) Keep Your Man*, *Staying Moist*, *Sex Yourself*, *Orgasm Weekly* and *The (Perfect) Blowjob* – followed the publishing trends of the 1980s and 1990s, until the editorial department was closed altogether in 2004 when the magazine became absorbed into *The Celebrity* along with another acquisition, *The Diet*, becoming *The Celebrity (with The Diet incorporating The (Perfect) Blowjob)*.

woman would feel better for having control over. Foundation, of the kind we can buy with ease nowadays at Boots, was unheard of then; well, perhaps not unheard of, but it was at least unavailable even for those of us who had access to a private income to supplement our wages. For working-class girls it was beyond imagining! A homemade alternative – a mixture of gravy browning and cordite – was popular with the more 'ready' sort of working-class girl, but it held several disadvantages. For example, it could 'run' in the rain, leaving a face and collar streaked, or even disappear altogether if the girl's face were licked. Under certain conditions it could explode, blowing a lady's cheeks off. Also, the cordite had an unpleasant odour that not even the best French perfume could mask.

I knew of no one within my social circle who used it, and I personally had never tried it because I was then only eighteen years of age, and although sometimes my freckles made me quite cross I still knew my skin to be taut, smooth and attractive. It had a fresh, soft quality with the faintest of bloom (quite natural, I'm happy to say!) across the cheeks. At school I had been the envy of my entire dormitory, not needing even an occasional dab of cold cream to maintain a creamy complexion without dryness or flaking.

So I hurried towards work with my face *au naturel*, as the French would say on the Parisian boulevards, and did so with great anticipation, for this was to be my very first job since leaving Cheltenham Ladies' College. I remember that I had butterflies in my tummy as I left the Underground at Green Park and began to thread my way through side streets towards New Bond Street. Really, I was so excited that I can remember every step I took as though it were just a few hours ago, rather than twenty-six years!

I had my father's permission to take the position; in fact I had his blessing as it was he who had suggested it to me after he heard about it from Uncle Mole. (Of course, Uncle 'Mole' wasn't his real name! However, my lovable Uncle Reginald had always reminded me of a cuddly, sweet, furry mole, being quite rotund and having a lot of facial twitching, and as a little girl I had always clambered onto his lap and laughed gaily as I tried to rub my own tiny snub nose against his much larger twitching one! It became something of a family joke at first, and then later a tradition, and I was still clambering onto his lap and pressing my face lovingly into his until only minutes before his death from pleurisy last year.)

News of the position had come to Uncle Mole on what he called 'the jungle telegraph'. I didn't understand what that was, at first, and although he tried to explain it several times it always eluded me until eventually he said that it wasn't that important and that we should move on.

I arrived at the offices of S.T.A.S. (or 'Esters' as we who worked there all called it, although '*The Selman-Troytt Appreciation Society*' was its proper, grand title!) at 8:25 – thirty-five minutes early – because I was keen to make a good first impression. After all, it was my first day! Unfortunately, there was no one else there, but a kindly man from the building superintendent's office let me in and I busied myself with a little light dusting and then re-sharpened all the pencils I had brought with me. (I had recently finished a course in Pitman's Shorthand and never went anywhere without a clean notebook and two gross* of pencils.) I remember the dust had a kind of greasy quality to it because I smudged some on the *broderie Anglaise* edging of the puff-sleeve of my taffeta dress and was unable to blow or brush it away. Instead it clung on, with that kind of tenacity that makes one's heart absolutely sink because one knows that one will be reaching for soap and water any second and will very likely leave an unremovable [*sic*] mark. How's that for a start to my day, I thought crossly. What will they think of me now! It was any girl's worst nightmare.

At 9 o'clock Mr. Finlayson arrived, accompanied by his personal assistant Margot Churton-Kurdost, daughter of the Derbyshire Churton-Kurdosts and a really well-known debutante! And with all of her own teeth! I remembered her photograph very well from the front pages of '*The Debutante*' just two seasons before. How I envied her

* One gross = 144 pencils

beautiful dress and graceful carriage. She had absolutely marvellous deportment, with a lithe body that seemed to drape and move sinuously in a graceful ballet whose rhythm was never once impeded by a firm, well-shaped and heavenly-sized bust that would make every woman on earth absolutely green with envy! Honestly, on anyone else it would have looked clumsy or gauche, whereas on her it just added to her allure and gave her appeal such potency that none could fail to feel it! She was *so* blessed! I think I was in absolute awe of her from that first minute.

I watched her climb the office steps then turn on the top one to wait for Mr. Finlayson to ascend them also. I remember that the bright morning sun seemed to make her summer frock translucent as she stood tall and effortlessly straight, her slender, shapely legs just slightly apart to encourage the soft, cooling touches of any summer breezes that circled teasingly. He beautiful blond hair, fired by sunlight, became a golden halo that shrouded her head and whose rays seemed to fill the hallway with golden ambience. She was so goddess-like that I remember experiencing a very powerful surge of affection for her, just as one might for one's older sister whom one admires very much, and I had a sudden urge to clamber on to her lap and laugh with her as we rubbed noses in intimate play – which would scarcely have 'done' on my first day, of course! Years later, when we were friendly enough to clamber onto each other's laps all the time, she would laugh at my recollections and call me a 'silly goose' whilst she gave me an affectionate nibble on the earlobe. I never took offence; I knew she meant it kindly.

Wanting to show myself willing, I went out from behind my desk and stood on the front steps just behind Margot. I peeped out from behind the radiance of her hair and caught my first glimpse of Mr. Finlayson. He was making the very slow journey from the taxi-cab to the first step, bravely crossing the pavement without walking aids, and unaware that the diaphanous material of his post-war trousers clung to the contours of his legs, showing their tiny dimensions. I remember feeling amazed that any torso could be supported on legs so thin. It seemed that they must snap at any moment, so frail did they look, and a wave of sympathy rose up in me and threatened to bring tears to my eyes. To save myself from embarrassment I coughed very loudly and offered to make everyone a nice cup of tea.

By the time it was brewed, Margot had gently guided Mr. Finlayson up the steps, through the entrance hall, and into the main office, and he was very nearly at a chair upon which he could rest before undertaking the second leg of his journey into his office proper. Margot was absolutely marvellous with him – knowing just when to encourage or scold, just when to hold and guide, and just when to release him so that he could try a few steps unaided. I could tell at a glance that all her actions went beyond mere duty, so caring were they, and this was confirmed over the weeks and months that followed. She never left his side, and often volunteered to remain late in his office if there was important archiving work to do. I like to think she may have been a little in love with him – which is a wonderfully romantic image: her being the demure debutante and he the returning heroic airman – but it is unlikely that she was, when you consider her youth, exquisite beauty and wealth weighed against his age, his appearance and the fragility of his legs. But, still, I like to think it! And she *was* marvellous with him, always opening the books he wanted to read and then turning the pages when he couldn't do it for himself. Again and again, with no sign of impatience; she was an angel. Certainly I know that my own respect and affection for her increased as the months went by and I saw her nurture him through the worst of his incapacities. As he grew stronger, so did their bond, until she became elevated to a position of such status within the Association that she became the *de facto* head of personnel, taking it upon her own shoulders to find for him assistants with the necessary charm, skill and breeding to ease his daily passage through life and work. I admired her tremendously, and I'm not sure I ever stopped looking up to her.

My first day was very busy, even a little overwhelming, as I dealt with several pieces of correspondence – pounding out the letters on a pre-war Remington – and orchestrated the comings and goings of several visitors (the postman, the stationer and the meter reader) and had to rise to the challenge of remembering the location of everything from carbon paper to the custard creams that Margot fed to Mr. Finlayson.

At last, lunchtime arrived, carrying with it a heady aroma of cabbage

[Some omitted here. Ed.*]*

which caused the streetlights to dim all along Piccadilly.

By that time, almost three months later, he was using the bath chair only when he couldn't go another step. Then he would suddenly shout for it, and then flop back into it with a loud gasp the second he felt it touch the back of his calves. Cynthia, who had joined just after Alice but had never known her at Badminton, although they shared adjoining dormitories apparently, would then tuck a blanket around his legs to conceal his lap from passers by. She did it out of loyalty and respect.

We all thought he worked too hard. Through long days he would sit reading, cataloguing or note-taking – by dictation sometimes, or by hand if he thought his fingers were strong enough for a pen – and by nights he laboured over the Herculean task of trying to editorialise the work of Mr. Selman-Troytt. And there was so much of it! The office was absolutely full of it, and more was arriving daily in trucks. It was very difficult work – even thinking about Mr. Finlayson doing it used to make my own head spin! – and every week my respect for him grew. Often he took no proper nourishment, seeming to exist on a diet of custard creams softened in weak tea. I thought him frightfully brave and clever. And still do!

And his work didn't finish with his academic labours, for there were increasing numbers of receptions to attend, speeches to give, interviews to grant, articles to write, and members to welcome as the work of Jeremy Selman-Troytt began to spread around the globe and his popularity began to surge. And guess who was responsible for orchestrating much of it? That's right – I'd come a long way from that first day with a smudge on my sleeve and those funny, awkward feelings in my lower tummy!

Soon, letters began to arrive from the most exotic of places. I remember one from Peru – I used to save the stamps for my nephew, Harold, who hoped to re-use them so that he could cut down on postage costs – and we all gathered around it and gasped. It would be almost commonplace now, I suppose, but in those days it was more excitement than many of the girls could take. Several had to go to the lavatory in pairs.

It went on that way for some time. And we were able to meet some truly amazing people. Senator McCarthy came in one time, and then Mr. Khrushchev. And Tom Jones came in with Ted Moult. And Professor Ravensbury, Charles Singleton, P.J. Proby, Bernard Levin and The Beatles all stopped by at various times! The day The Beatles came it was as though time stood still. One minute they weren't there; and the next they were! We were all just completely overwhelmed. They were suddenly just standing in the main reception room, looking around cheekily, just like you'd see them do on television. We were all just overwhelmed. Andrea suddenly lost control of her bladder, so we all coughed loudly to cover the noise of it and began offering them custard creams to distract them from the mess.

My favourite in those days was Paul, and I hardly knew where to put my eyes when he moved closer. I was so grateful when he stared straight through me to spare me embarrassment.

After they went in to join Mr. Finlayson we just stood in the outer office and shook our heads with numb disbelief, partly due to their sudden appearance and partly because Ringo's nose was somehow even bigger in real life than it appeared on film. Davinia made an off-colour remark about the many uses to which it could be put, and one of the juniors laughed but we were too shocked to scold her properly. The rapid changes we had just experienced were too much for some girls and I heard sniffles as they began to decompress.

On another occasion the Prime Minister, Harold Wilson, came in, but it wasn't as exciting.

By 1968 we were so busy that there were suggestions made that we should move offices. Some of the girls were very excited about the prospect of moving to more spacious accommodation, especially those whom Mr. Finlayson often kept behind late for archiving, but I felt a stab of regret at leaving somewhere that had become a second home for me. The next day, an estate agent called wearing a lounge suit that was rather *louche*. He had a pencil moustache of the kind I'd not seen since a black-marketeer had tried to sell some stolen pork to my father over the garden wall in 1944, a manner that was oleaginous and nauseating, and hands that were everywhere! Within minutes of his arrival I could feel the tips of his fingers gently probing the sensitive ridges of my

[Remainder omitted. Ed.*]*

Appendix V

O'Rourke & LeFevre – Pioneers in Print

(From An Introduction to Progressive Publishing *by Professor A. A. R. Burton-Mills, used by kind permission of the author)*

The publishing house of O'Rourke & LeFevre has been at the vanguard of progressive publishing for so long now that it needs no formal introduction here. A household name for more than seven decades, it has seeped deeply into the public consciousness, and whether one is a florist, a surgeon, a drill sergeant, a spelunker, an orthodontist or a proctologist one is likely to have held an O'Rourke & LeFevre publication in one's hands for instruction, stimulation or amusement. The company's rise to publishing pre-eminence since its foundation in 1851 by Pat O'Rourke and Jean LeFevre has been well-catalogued in numerous journals, yet the facts behind the company's formation are equally fascinating.

Pat[rick] O'Rourke was born in Dublin in 1830, the third of eleven children of various sexes. His father, Seamus O'Rourke, was a printer, publisher, pamphleteer, and a vendor of seditious tracts at markets and travelling shows. Intermittently he worked as a varnish stirrer at the Cambellgrove Sealant Works on the banks of the Liffey, and frequently had hands so heavily coated with varnish that no amount of solvent would unstiffen them. He came home only very rarely, and when he did was invariably surprised at the numbers of children in his house, in part because his wife had denied him intercourse since the third week of their marriage. Pat's earliest memories of his father are of 'an occasional visitor with claw-like hands encased in a thick brown shiny carapace. He was unable to turn the doorknob for himself . . .'

The O'Rourke family's connection with the seditious, 'darker' side of printing and publishing stretched back several generations to when Pat's great-great-great-grandfather, Churchill O'Rourke, had been offered 'first refusal' on Swift's *A Modest Proposal** during a clandestine meeting in the upper rooms of The Bouncing Anglican alehouse in O'Connell Street. To maintain their *incognito* all participants had agreed to come in disguise, and though Swift contented himself with a hooded cloak Churchill had come dressed as a beagle. A relentlessly literal man, who often boasted that 'no dreams could take root in a brain like mine', he read *A Modest Proposal* while Swift waited, but signally failed to note the irony in it. Instead, he read it as a very serious proposal that children should be eaten, and became incensed and emotional at their sufferings. Ignoring the objections of others present, he punched Swift repeatedly in the face until he was unrecognisable.

Swift was apoplectic with rage at the incident and shortly thereafter confided to Pope and Arbuthnot** by letter:

> This confirms to me that the Irish be both awkward and pernicious. The gulley of ambivalence I felt towards them hitherto has deepened into a gorge, and I am like to throw myself into it. I never thought to hate them as I do but the vice bites deep within me.

Churchill was deeply contrite when the mistake was explained to him, and invited Swift to punch him senseless in return. Swift availed himself of the offer on the evening of 11th November, and then again on 15th

* A satirical pamphlet written by Jonathan Swift in 1729. At the time, Swift was Dean of St Patrick's Cathedral in Dublin.

** Alexander Pope (author of *The Rape of the Lock*) and John Arbuthnot (physician and satirist) were lifelong friends of Swift. Like him, both were extremely short, the tallest of the group being Arbuthnot at 4'6" (1.30m).

and 20th of the same month. He booked a further session for the following January. He later wrote to Pope:

> Although I could feel my knuckles bruising against his head, and could not in consequence hold even my pen for some weeks afterwards, I cannot describe the ecstasy that flowed through me and which enriched my soul with a warmth of release that seemed to transport me. In his pain, and in my own, I found a release far beyond that which I have ever known with Stella.*

This episode marked the end of the relationship between Churchill and Swift, the latter already angered by Churchill's reaction to *Gulliver's Travels* four years before. Churchill had been impressed by the descriptions, but had mistaken it for a genuine travel guide and was bothered by the lack of maps.

Summarising his publishing career on his death bed, he stated:

> I suppose if there was a nemesis at all in my life then irony was your man! It used to come at me sideways, always bobbing and weaving. I never could tell the false bits to be read as true, from the true bits to be read as false. Or is it the other way around?

Successive generations of O'Rourkes fared better, and by the early nineteenth century Pat's father, Seamus, was an enthusiastic publisher of anti-British propaganda. Occasionally, when Ireland proved too hot

* 'Stella' was Swift's nickname for Esther Johnson, at various times his ward, friend and live-in companion. Their relationship was ambiguous and remains largely impenetrable to most scholars. Many modern literary biographers argue that their relationship was platonic, but then often stumble when forced to reconcile such a theory with several of the 'potentially intimate' references made by Esther Johnson in letters to her close friend Rebecca Dingley, such as: 'When [Jonathan] is too tired to ejaculate in his own hand, he ejaculates in mine.'

for him, he would flee abroad, often finding succour in other centres of agitation such as Paris.

It was on one such journey in 1845 that he met Simon-Paul LeFevre, father of Jean, in a meeting that would later have great significance for their children.

The LeFevres also had several generations of anti-establishment publishing experience behind them. Simon-Paul's father, Paul-Simon, had risked imprisonment many times in order to publish anti-monarchist tracts prior to the French revolution of 1789. His work was dangerous, but he was spurred on by the hatred he felt for those in power. In fact, such repugnance did he hold for authority, and such sympathy for the underdog, that after the revolution he switched to publishing pro-royalist material and began trying to undermine the new republic.

By the time Seamus appeared in Paris, Simon-Paul was part of a well-established group of subversives prepared to denounce anyone who wielded the slightest power, even members of their own group. The two men met first in a modest café and exchanged stories and news over wine and food. That night began a friendship which continued via written correspondence for the rest of their lives.

Upon his return to Dublin, and remembering Simon-Paul's passing mention of his own fourteen-year-old child Jean, Seamus urged the fifteen-year-old Pat to strike up a correspondence of his own so as to broaden the boy's mind.

And so began the historic correspondence between Pat and Jean. The letters are now preserved in the 'O'Rourke Collection' at the Smithsonian Institution and provide wonderful insights into the genesis of this famous relationship.

Their first attempts at communication were halting because Pat had no French and Jean was familiar only with the English word 'cusp'. However, each persevered alone because neither wanted to subject their confidences to parental scrutiny. After several false starts they settled on using the only language they had in common: Latin. Their knowledge of the language was not extensive, but both children had been in the hands of Jesuits at one time or another for some modest classical scholarship, and both attended regular church services conducted in Latin.

Their earliest exchanges are fascinating, if occasionally confusing to the uninitiated, and have long been a source of academic study. Unsurprisingly, given their youth and lack of education, there are errors of syntax and grammar, as well as lapses of vocabulary and intelligibility. Nevertheless, for two untrained and ill-educated correspondents they show great literary courage.

Professor Madden of Christ's College, Cambridge is a world-renowned expert on the letters and has been studying them since 1961. He has been kind enough to provide some translated samples from their exchanges. It should be noted that these examples are from the 'A' folio, where Professor Madden has translated *verbatim* from the Latin where writing is legible, and has attempted elucidation where there is ambiguity.

Dublin, 26 May 1845

Dear Jean,

I have [a] dog. Black. Laddie [is] his name. Laddie by [or with] spoons. Spoons you? Herein thus mist father too. And the spoons of you? Dog we [unreadable] black? I love all animals. I like to push [pet(?)] their heads.

Yours with grace and demeanour,
Pat

Paris, 18 June 1845

Dear Pat

Yes – I adore of which the spoons. I adore him always. He advises the blank face of [unreadable] house citizens. Do you laugh? Yours is by [or with] temerity. Mine is by [or with] my father, always elixir. Mother never. I hold the spoons of my father.

With grace and demeanour,
Jean

What is particularly interesting, from a linguistic or philological perspective, is the use of the word 'spoons' in so many contextual permutations throughout their letters (it occurs seven hundred and sixteen times in eighty-three letters). Clearly the word is not used 'legitimately' to mean 'spoons', as you or I might use it, and therefore constitutes an 'error' semiologically speaking; but, equally clearly, it has a *shared meaning*, or perhaps we might rather state that it *developed a shared meaning*, between these correspondents. Therefore, it presents us with an interesting and ironic paradox, insofar as it could be argued, semiologically at least, that any word which carries 'meaning' or 'signification' within a context understood by participants must not, *ipso facto*, constitute 'illegitimate' or 'erroneous' language. Fascinating!

Reading through the letters in sequence it is possible to mark not only a burgeoning friendship and affection as the participants grow older, but also an increase in their confidence as they become more comfortable within the relationship. What also becomes increasingly clear is that each man thought the other to be a woman.

How this confusion arose is not wholly clear, but in an age before photography, and with both boys keen to keep their correspondence and relationship private, we must conclude that their simple mistake was founded upon the assumption each made about the other's Christian name. This appears confirmed by Pat O'Rourke's autobiography, written many years later, which records: "It never occurred to me, not even once, that 'Jean' would be anything but a girl with a name like that. I mean, wasn't one of my own aunts called 'Jean'? But the joke was on me, after all; and a big, cruel bastard of joke it was too. There I was, fantasising every night about a 'her' in flouncey white petticoats, when all the while it was this great hairy-arsed bollix with heavy side-whiskers. Sure, life is a joke that forces you to laugh your way to the surface . . . if it doesn't drown you first in sadness."*

As years passed, their correspondence continued rhythmically and their affection became more ardent. Phrases such as 'I yearn for your arms', 'I love you', 'One day (of *not* tomorrow) I kiss of spoons', and 'with all adoration of the hearts' attest to their deepening feelings. It is unclear when those feelings first deepened fully into love, but when the subject of marriage arose in correspondence of May 1850, both leaped at the chance to take their relationship to its logical conclusion.

However, both being still below the age of majority, and knowing they were unlikely to obtain parental consent for a liaison in which the participants had never met, the twenty-year-old Pat agreed impulsively to elope with the nineteen-year-old Jean, each firmly believing they would be journeying into the future with the woman who inspired their adolescent dreams. Pat, as the oldest, agreed to travel to Paris.

Taking his meagre savings, and filling his pockets with enough cheese to sustain him on the journey, Pat set off without telling Seamus of his departure, travelling from Dublin to Brittany by fishing smack. He then made his way overland to Paris and installed himself as arranged in the Hotel Crouton in Montparnasse.

From there he sent the following by special messenger:

> *Dearest Jean,*
>
> *[Acropos(?)] Hotel Crouton. There is [are] spoons tubular concession [unreadable]. I yearn your hands. Yearn you loving darling? You I hold in my mind and you are in my eyes. I see your spoons and am without breath. Our meeting can be where and when?*

---

* *From Cellar to Seller – Fifty Years in Publishing*, Pat O'Rourke, O'Rourke & LeFevre, Dublin, 1896, pp 67–68

Waiting is difficult! I am not able. Inform me. My breath disappears.

All my love and my heart is fast,
Pat xxxxxxxxxxxxxx

The reply came swiftly:

Dearest Pat,

You arrive! You arrive! You arrive! Your name sings in my ears. I love you! You are so near. [Unreadable] corduroy? Yes, certainly of the spoons! Naturally!! All my spoons!!!! Why not, if we are married? Oh, I love you! Yes, I yearn your hands!! Every day in dreams. I have my baggage in a bag and ready only your letter. Tomorrow we meet. Place Pradeau. At ten hours the morning. I love you!!!!!!!!!!

Jean xxxxxxxxxxxxxxxx
xxxxxxxxxxxxxxxxxxxx
xxxxxxxxxxxxxxxxxxxx

The anticipation felt by each man is abundantly clear in these letters, and we know that they planned to meet, embrace quickly and then flee straight to the Seine where they would rent a boat to take them to Troyes. Once there, they hoped to marry in the shadow of the fountain and then quickly consummate their union in the nearest *pension*.

The following morning found them both on the crowded Place Pradeau, eagerly scanning the passing crowds for their first sight of a woman clutching a large baguette draped with a tricolour – the signal of recognition upon which they had already agreed.

We can try to empathise with their feelings of joy, optimism and excitement as each waited to catch sight of the woman whose imagined softness and beauty had stirred his imaginings through a thousand fevered and lonely nights. In fact, when one considers the high pitch of expectation to which their imaginations had already brought them, subsequent events become much more understandable. For realisation, when it arrived, must have struck with a force and suddenness sufficient to shatter their dreams in an instant. Certainly the rapid transition from exhilaration to devastation left both men stupefied as they finally came face to face and stared at the flag-draped baguette in the other's hand. That dramatic, cruel intervention by reality momentarily robbed both men of their senses. LeFevre described the sensation as 'akin to being blown along in a huge storm', while O'Rourke found it 'similar to breathing in fumes from a blast furnace'.

But within O'Rourke the confusion was quickly joined by a frequent companion: anger. Instantly he felt himself deceived, deprived and bereft. And while the gentler LeFevre simply continued to gape in open-mouthed astonishment at the red-faced, heavy-set and bearded man who came in the guise of his fiancée, it was O'Rourke who allowed his Celtic passions to overrule his finer sensibilities and unleash the demons within him.

Focusing on the object of his delusions he leapt forward with a bellow of rage and head-butted LeFevre in the centre of the face with enough force to break both of his cheekbones and explode his nose. In fact, so extensive was the damage that LeFevre suffered a maxillary depression and developed an adenoidal impediment so severe that his speech became all but incomprehensible thereafter.

The blow was immense, the sound of the impact echoing around the square, and bystanders related how Jean fell to the ground, screaming inconsolably with the pain while Pat stood over him breathing heavily. 'More than anything else, it was that screaming,' O'Rourke wrote later, 'that awoke me to the enormity of what I had done. I looked at him lying there broken, the person with whom I had shared so much for so long, and something within me broke too. It was more than remorse. It was a kind of self-hatred for the loathsome, pride-filled vermin I saw myself to be. I never felt so low, so disgusted, as I was at that second. I wanted to wipe myself from the earth. The thought of Jean so injured, and me so whole, was suddenly insupportable to me. If I could not restore him, I reasoned, then the very least I could do was shatter myself similarly to make amends in the eyes of God. I felt an ungovernable urge to destroy myself in the same way. In a fury I cast about me, searching for the nearest wall so I could run my face into it.'*

Witnesses gave various accounts of what happened next, but all agree that they saw a large, red-faced man take off at a charging run that took him through an ornamental flowerbed, across the road, and up against a nearby house. Unfortunately for O'Rourke, his stampeding run brought him not against the blank section of wall that would have shattered his nose, but against a jutting section of window ledge that shattered his lower jaw instead. The top corner of the ledge caught him just at the level of his upper teeth, snapping them off in an instant, and so great was his momentum that his forward motion was stopped only when the ledge made stout contact with his larynx. The impact devastated his lower jaw, breaking it into forty-three separate pieces 'that swayed and jumbled under my face in a kind of sloppy bag that hung limply against my neck. What became of my teeth is anyone's guess. When I awoke it was to find that my entire lower jaw had, for all practical purposes, disappeared. I knew then that my kissing days were over. Amazingly, my nose had not even so much as a scratch on it, which only goes to show!'**

Both men were moved into the care of a physician at the Salpêtrière, but there was little he could do beyond allowing the wounds to heal themselves. Faced with such extensive injury he made some attempts to keep their airways clear, but facial reconstruction was out of the question and both men were left with the consequences of that day's meeting. LeFevre awoke to find that 'the centre of my face was a misshapen mass that never again admitted air or smell', while for O'Rourke the sobering news was that his food would need to be pureed

---

* ibid., p.89

** ibid., p.94

henceforth. What was left of his jaw was allowed to heal into 'a kind of leathery bag that became harder and smaller and chafed on my neck as years went by'.* Both men were unable to speak properly and could do nothing but follow the doctor's recommendation to wait for improvement. O'Rourke's prognosis was the less optimistic of the two, as he was without a lower jaw, and indeed for the rest of his life he was never able to progress beyond the utterance of a series of grunts that changed in pitch and frequency as he became more excited.

Understandably, their thoughts on subsequent pain-filled days were dark ones, for at a stroke each man had lost physical functionality, a fiancée, and the words to try and find a replacement. Both men were evidently depressed, and O'Rourke's autobiography states: 'I am not sure if I was unhappy, as such, but I did want to kill myself'**. In addition to concerns about his own physical welfare, O'Rourke was also tortured by guilt at what he had done to Jean. Over the weeks that followed, this sense of self-recrimination was eased only by Jean's assertions that he did not hold Pat to blame. He attempted to emphasise this forgiveness by feeding his erstwhile fiancée a little bouillon through a tube.

Over the next few weeks their emotions stabilised and their earlier regard for each other began to re-emerge. As LeFevre said later: 'What was interesting is how we felt about each other. We were not pederasts but in a very curious way we loved each other dearly. For me, Pat was just a woman in a man's body. It is impossible to be as intimate as we had been hitherto and not develop a lasting love. It was only a shame that we could not express our feelings physically in order to consummate our affair, but it was impossible given our gender and our religion.'

It was a full three months until they were ready to leave the hospital, by which time they had repaired their relationship to a significant degree. Upon discharge they made for the protection of Seamus in

---

* ibid., p.103

** ibid., p.104

Dublin and once in the city they attempted to reassemble their lives.

[*Section omitted here. Details of the subsequent formation of O'Rourke & LeFevre in Dublin, and of Pat and Jean's burgeoning personal and business relationship between 1850 and 1900, are well-documented in scores of texts and have therefore been removed from this account*. Ed.]

As their wealth increased, so did the grandeur of their accommodations. By the time of their deaths they inhabited the picturesque 'Drogh'gannogh' estate to the north of Dublin, where Pat, who was opposed to blood sports, would have pheasants shot in a box to avoid unnecessary spattering.

For more than fifty years they enjoyed the satisfaction of being in each other's company, working together during the day and spending the evenings playing chess, or other non-verbal games. Pat would sit of an evening, filled with a sense of wonder at the beauty of the setting sun, whilst Jean never lost interest in watching Pat trying to smoke a pipe.

They both died in 1903, Jean first and Pat a few weeks later, partly from loneliness but mostly because Jean had misplaced his feeding tube. The firm they founded continues to go from strength to strength, and now has offices in every major city on earth.

Appendix VI

The 'Glazing Wars' – Economic Causes & Geo-Political Effects

A political and economical analysis by Finlay Finlayson, B.A. (Oxon.) F.S.T.A.S.

Sitting in the tranquillity of my offices, on a drowsy, warm summer's afternoon such as this one, with the distant traffic of Piccadilly no more than a muted rumble, it seems impossible for me to comprehend that a scant seventy years* separates the comforting order of a contented post-war Britain from the chaos and upheaval that typified the closing decades of the last century.

Those tumultuous years did much to shape the world as we know it today, and they continue to touch the lives of everyone, even indirectly. For example, many people alive today have relatives (assuming they are alive also) who experienced those events *first-hand* – a fact that still surprises me every time I consider it. My own grandfather, for instance, although now long dead, once bought a piece of glass for five shillings** from a printer's assistant in a toilet stall in Euston station and sold it three hours later for eighteen shillings† to a costermonger in Kent. Both transactions occurred in 1882.

However, it should be noted clearly at the outset that the economic/

---

* This piece first appeared in *The Observer* on 11th August 1953.

** 25p

† 90p

political phenomenon to which modern historians often refer (mistakenly) as the 'Glazing Wars of the 1890s' was actually a series of commercial manoeuvres and activities that began *very much* earlier in the century, and which had their roots in the demography and fiscal trends of the mid-nineteenth century. It should also be borne in mind that had those events not occurred, and had the Selman-Troytt family not become significantly enriched by them, then much of Jeremy's research work would not be available to us now, for it was funded by family donations. Try, if you will, to imagine a world bereft of that richness. I try, often, and am unable; for it lies beyond the shores of my comprehension. It is the equivalent of trying to imagine the world without telescopes (through which our horizons are extended) or warm clothing, or tinned food. Once seen, it becomes impossible to *un-see*.

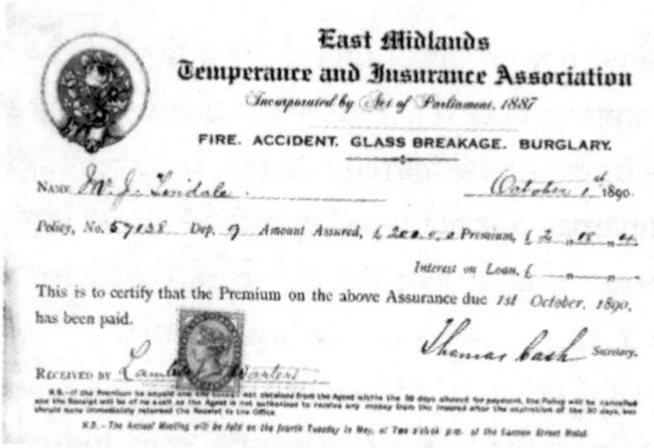

East Midlands
Temperance and Insurance Association
Incorporated by Act of Parliament, 1887

FIRE. ACCIDENT. GLASS BREAKAGE. BURGLARY.

NAME *Mr. J. Lindale* *October 1st* 1890.

Policy, No. *57138* Dep. *9* Amount Assured, £ *200.0.0* Premium, £ *2.18.4*

Interest on Loan, £ — — —

This is to certify that the Premium on the above Assurance due *1st October, 1890*, has been paid.

Thomas Cash Secretary.

RECEIVED BY

Everyday life in the Victorian England of 1850 was much as we know it today (excepting the convenience of modern things like aeroplanes, televisions, radios, toothpaste, Vaseline, Bakelite, Vim and torpedoes, obviously) in the sense that there was a predictability to existence that must have been a great comfort to those living at that time. No one likes to live not knowing what will happen from one second to the next because it can lead to confusion and . . .

[*The remainder of this essay, charting the rising fortunes of the Selman-Troytt family and their part in the manipulations of the glazing markets, can be found on the website for the Selman-Troytt Appreciation Society (*www.selman-troytt.com*).* Ed.]

Appendix VII

Selman-Troytt's decision to advertise in the 'personal' columns of newspapers was made when his search for a wife was at its most intense. Frustrated by his inability to find a woman with the appropriate disposition, personality or pudenda within his own social circle, he regarded advertising as the perfect method for establishing compatibility with the minimum of time and cost.

The opportunity for pre-vetting and 'filtering' potential spouses excited him enormously, appealing both to his scientific bent and his preference for speaking as little as possible, and he was to run more than forty variations of such advertisements from 1906 to 1916.

The example below is from his first draft, and ran for thirty-seven consecutive weeks in *The Times*.

> Gentleman, 37, slim (in upper torso) intellectual *bon vivant*, interested in all matters scientific, of independent means and phlegmatic disposition, mild dyspepsia with occasional flatulence but otherwise sound constitution, seeks very similar lady (aged 18–24) with unblemished pudenda for marriage, procreation and experimental research. Must be of sound mind, clean habits and preferably without offensive odour. Non-talker preferred.
>
> *Apply Box 3872.*

A List of Works by Jeremy Selman-Troytt

(All titles are published by O'Rourke & LeFevre unless otherwise indicated.)

Preparing an Efficacious Poultice
Applying an Efficacious Poultice (Companion Work to the above)
Removing Poultice Stains
My Blood – What It Is and Why I Need It
Desquamation – Basic Flake Collection & Storage
The First Time I Soiled My Trousers – Part I
The First Time I Soiled My Trousers – Part II
A Study of Seepage
The Second Time I Soiled My Trousers
Reflections on Skin – A Study of Intensive Flaking
The Third Time I Soiled My Trousers
A Catalogue of Tumescence
The Fourth Time I Soiled My Trousers
Getting Through the Night – How to Sleep Peacefully With Others in the Room
Further Seepage
The Fifth Time I Soiled My Trousers
A Study of Working-Class Pudenda (Colour Plates)
The Search for a Perfect Lotion (Illustrated)
Speculations upon Improbable Joint Articulations
The Sixth Time I Soiled My Trousers
Patterns Of Sleep – 9,000 Detailed Observations Made Minute By Minute
Overcoming Natural Repugnance during Coition
The Seventh Time I Soiled My Trousers
Ear Measurements – A Comparison of 1000 Ears in a Blind Study
The Eighth Time I Soiled My Trousers
Another Catalogue of Tumescence
The Ninth Time I Soiled My Trousers
From Mouth To Rectum – A Journey through My Digestive Tract (Blackwell's 'Young Minds Science Series'), Blackwell Press, London, 1904
The Tenth Time I Soiled My Trousers
My Body Shape – Possible Contributory Factors
Erectile Dysfunction – 1,684 Recorded Observations of Detumescence
The Eleventh Time I Soiled My Trousers – Part I
The Case Against Involuntary Emasculation (monograph), New Scientist, Vol. xi, London.

The Eleventh Time I Soiled My Trousers – Part II
The Case Against Auto-Emasculation (monograph), New Scientist, Vol. xvi, London.
Re-establishing Memory after Slight Head Trauma
Examining Mr. Butterfield– Part I
The Eleventh Time I Soiled My Trousers – Part III
Examining Mr. Butterfield – Part II
Coping With Larger Legs
The Twelfth Time I Soiled My Trousers
Coping with Testicular Metamorphosis
From Bite to Bolus (Published In Germany as *How I Chew*) – 1202 Detailed Observations of Mastication & Swallowing
The Thirteenth Time I Soiled My Trousers
From Salve to Splint – Curing Erectile Dysfunction
The Fourteenth Time I Soiled My Trousers – Part I
My First Nocturnal Emission
The Fourteenth Time I Soiled My Trousers – Part II
My Second Nocturnal Emission
The Fourteenth Time I Soiled My Trousers – Part III
Seepage Re-Visited
Examining Mr. Butterfield – Part III
My Third Nocturnal Emission
The Fifteenth Time I Soiled My Trousers
My Fourth Nocturnal Emission
Repairing the Eyes – The Case For and Against
My Fifth Nocturnal Emission
My First Involuntary Emission
My Sixth Nocturnal Emission
Ensuring Procreation during Coition
The Sixteenth Time I Soiled My Trousers
Testicular Metamorphosis 1885–1911 (Published 1912)
Re-Establishing Binocular Vision after Concussion
My Seventh & Eighth Nocturnal Emissions
The Case Against Ingesting Putrid Foodstuffs
My Second Involuntary Emission
Curing Seepage – The Facts
A Comparison of Scrotal Movements within Conventional Ranges, 1870–1903 (Over 10,000 Detailed Observations Complete With Line Drawings.)
Curing Involuntary Ejaculation – The Facts
My Third Involuntary Emission
Curing Baldness – The Facts
My Fourth Involuntary Emission
The Search for a Portable Prepuce Retractor
My Fifth Involuntary Emission
Dressing in Women's Clothes: An Examination of Various Deviations
My Sixth Involuntary Emission
From Entry to Exit – Intercourse Explained & Justified
My Seventh Involuntary Emission
Are You Engaged For This Dance? – Preparing for the Possibility of Intercourse
Social and Sexual Etiquette – A Primer for All Adults

Bibliography

The following works were essential in the preparation on this volume:

The Serbian Problem – Another Problem That Won't Go Away, Jan Plckswnc, Belgrade, 1996

Unknown Causes of the Great War, Godfrey Shiner, Vanity Press, London, 2004

Through a Glass Darkly – A Study of Sharp Glazing Practices, Dr Mary Cockle, OUP, Oxford, 1971

Cloth Caps and Putty – The Unionisation of the Glazing Fraternity in Upper Silesia, H Clout, AGP, Bonn, 1999

The Unstoppable Chopper – Tree Felling and Parliamentary Debate: The Dual Life of W.E. Gladstone, Rikos Christodoulou, Olive Press, London, 2000

Practising Without a License, Jasper Selman-Troytt, O'Rourke & LeFevre, Dublin, 1902

Why Americans Are a Nuisance, Capel, Lewis, Rand, Scott, Douglas, Creamhorne, Dooley, Wilson, Leggatt, Legg, Leghorn, Lamb, Wenthrift, Cobb, Quill, Wisp, Coven, Pen, Chortle, Appleby, et al, Legation Press, London, 1997

Amusing Oneself When Women Are Talking (illus.), Cusper Dremh, Grench Gmbh, Frankfurt, 1988

Irony: Humorous Medium or Ferrous Discoloration? The questionable effect of comedic writing upon the ultra-literal in the U.S.A., L.V.V. Thomas R. Bender, United Gospel Church Press, Des Moines, 1987

A Dummy's Guide to Destabilising Russian Autocracies, H. Borowska, Freedom Books, Chechnya, 2002

Dressing for Success – The Contribution of Designer Clothing to Increasing Your Personal Fulfilment (16 pages – illustrated), Gretchen Luftbalon, Couture Press, London – Paris – Rome, 2005

Restabilising One's Life After Suicidal Depression, Dr. Randall H. Frewson, Exit Press, Solihull, 2004

Coping in a Boring Relationship, Jane and Peter Donne, Haricot Books, London, 2001

Disraeli's Greasy Pole – An Examination of Disraeli's Relationship with Queen Victoria, Heneker, Lansing, Bagnall, et al, Cambridge University Press, 1988

Trusting People Called Moynihan – Basic Dos and Don'ts, Ash Bourne & Paul Waters, Brixton Community Press, London, 1981

Living Without a Foreskin, Isaac R Levine, Doppler & Scissorvitch, London, 1960

Baccas, You Still Owe Me Forty Pounds for the Watch, Alex Jehovah, A B Press, Reading, 1991

Chewing the Fat – The Incomprehensible Attractiveness of Obese Partners, Billy-Bob Gruman Jr., Cellulite Press, Arkansas, 1988

Germans – Are They Worth the Trouble They Cause?, Rebecca McAlpine, Republican Books, Cork, 1962 (reprinted 43 times)

Last Exit to Brooklyn, Hubert Selby Jr., Grove Press, 1964

The Greenhouse Effect – Glazing Practices in Elizabethan England, Professor Sarah Lemcott, OUP, Oxford, 1968

Dying Painlessly Using the Proper Drugs, Herman Plectrum, Dover Educational Books, Dover, 2005

Curing Depression with Meditation, O. M. Mmm, Sekal Press, Kandahar, 2000

Hester's High Fibre Diet – Your Way to a Healthy Colon, Hester Pomade, Institutional Press, Brooklyn, 2006

The Legal Implications of Insurable Interest, Attorney Choices, Baptiste Press, London, 1981

Why the Irish Have All the Potatoes While the Arabs Have All the Oil – Geopolitical Realities Refracted Through Ironic Paradoxes, Gul Arif Shamar, Ketab Ketab, London, 2000

'Chubby Chasing' – Squeezing the Wheezing or Violent Contradiction?, Rev. Armand LeGrand, Garlic Press, Houston, 2002

'Shard – The weekly roundup of national news from the glazing industry', Editor: Peregrine Tint, Body Press, Winchester, Issues 204–4802.

Index

About the Editor

P.J. Barrington was born in Sai`thima, a remote Christian missionary station in Borneo, the son of a devout Scottish Presbyterian mother and an English sailor on leave. When her husband disappeared suddenly during morning prayers, Barrington's mother brought her infant son home to her native Mull where she continued her evangelical missionary work with a zeal undiminished by the fact that the islanders had been converted to Christianity more than a thousand years before.

Barrington was educated very locally, attending both Mull Elementary and Mull Comprehensive schools. At the latter he matriculated eventually with grades high enough to gain entry into Mull University, where he read for a BA in 'Local Customs and Geography of Tobermory'.

He is presently writing a thesis entitled 'The History of Mull, Past and Present'.